English Express Trains

[ONE SHILLING]

2 Papers

on

Express Trains

by

E. Foxwell

London:

EDWARD STANFORD, 55, CHARING CROSS, S.W.

1884.

[ONE SHILLING]

2 Papers

on

by

E. Foxwell

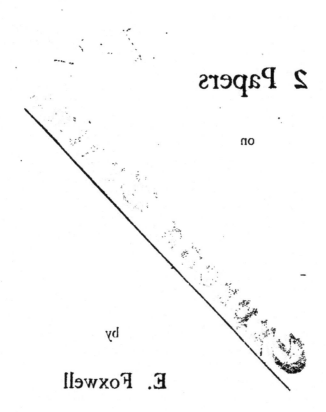

London:
EDWARD STANFORD, 55, CHARING CROSS, S.W.
1884.

ENGLISH

EXPRESS TRAINS:

TWO PAPERS

BY

E. FOXWELL.

LONDON:

EDWARD STANFORD, 55, CHARING CROSS, S.W.

1884.

NOTE.

———

THE following pages consist of two papers (more or less enlarged) which appeared, the first in *Macmillan's Magazine* for February 1883, and the second in the *Journal* of the Statistical Society, September 1883.

I have to thank Messrs. Macmillan for the liberty to publish the first, and am indebted to the Council of the Statistical Society for permission to reprint the second paper.

It may seem a medley to mix panegyric with statistics. But most Englishmen take an interest in the speed of express trains; and while the second of these papers offers an account of that speed, the first is meant to give some of the reasons why it is so interesting a subject.

The first paper is one-sided. Only the *good* results of speed are examined. Whatever injurious effects are caused by Railways, these are more properly the concern of the President of the Board of Trade than of any private person.

I must also express my thanks to the officials of the various Railway Companies for their very great courtesy in supplying me with information without which the second paper could not have been written.

E. F.

Cambridge, March, 1884.

CONTENTS.

———◆———

A 2

2nd Paper : STATISTICS (pp. 59—120).

EXPRESS TRAINS—AN APOLOGY.

I.

SHOULD there happen to be any Englishman

> " Who never to himself hath said,
>   ' This is my own, my native, land ! ' "

let him cultivate expresses. He will not emerge from this study
without a more intelligent affection for the island where railways
first appeared. His country is indeed one that might be defined as
the land of express trains, and such a definition would not be
accidental; for the qualities that gave rise to railway speed are
the very essence of English character.

And if we wish to know a nation well, we cannot do better
than examine one of its characteristic institutions. Now express
trains are *par excellence* the expression of English nature. When
we observe them we are feeling the pulse of the people in these
islands, and we ought to come away from the inspection with a
vivid diagnosis of our countrymen's disposition.

Railways a Cordial.

But apart from this, who can help admiring a perennial
exhibition of good spirits, and a sturdy performance of excellent
work—work which is in constant progress whether times are good
or bad? The country may be going to the dogs—in City papers—
but our railways go on better every year, inhaling stimulus from
every aspect. During the last ten years, a period of lamentation
among commercial men, railway improvement has advanced " by
" leaps and bounds," or rather by an incessant daily progress.
Steel rails have replaced iron almost everywhere, double lines have
become quadruple, hundreds of miles of siding have been added,
new carriages of a costlier kind have appeared in great numbers,
continuous breaks were the exception and are now the rule, inter-
locking has been adopted by the poorest companies, Liverpool and
Manchester have forged a third link of communication, the Midland

has established its mountain venture* to Carlisle, opened another
express route through Nottingham, and built the Severn Bridge;
the South Western has pushed round Dartmoor to Plymouth; a
very important line has been inserted between March and Lincoln,
and another half completed between Didcot and Southampton; the
Severn and Mersey tunnels have been made practicable; while an
unusual amount of work has been done in the construction of first-
class stations, such as those of Bristol, York, Tynemouth, Liverpool,†
Manchester,† Carlisle, Devonport,‡ and Liverpool Street. During
these same ten years there has been an extraordinary increase both
of expresses and of their speed (thanks to Bessemer rails); more
passengers have been carried faster and more safely; through
bookings have spread in every direction; cushions and third-class
have become inseparable; and for improved facilities we may
instance a case like that of Liverpool and Manchester, whose
express communication with each other has more than doubled,
and with London grown 30 per cent., since 1873; while the Great
Northern has kept on outstripping itself, the Great Eastern has
admirably shed its old skin, and the big Great Western has nearly
completed a similar change. Most industries have had a fit of
"the blues," but railways, depending upon all, have been busy in
these hypochondriac years with more sterling improvement than
in any former period of similar length. Finding themselves in a
"depression," they made it a stimulus to their undertakings. Then,
having set up new permanent way and built better carriages, they
proceeded to encourage the public with fresh editions of expresses.
Two or three companies—and notably the Great Eastern§—played
the part of physician to their country. Knowing that in such
times it is not the goods but their makers who are at fault, they
exhibited their dose of new speed or new facility to tempt the
patient, and so succeeded in drawing out energy when it was not
on the surface. We have to thank the Great Eastern in particular
for showing that the "dynamic" view of human beings may lead
to financial success.

This unfailing tonic property of our great railways makes them
a specially attractive study. They are always in a state of advance,
though the air they breathe may be dark with demoralisation.
When the country is prostrate with commercial ague, these com-

---

* Blea Moor tunnel is 1,130, and Ais Gill Sidings 1,170, feet above sea level.
† "Central" stations.
‡ L. & S.W.
§ In the late depression no Company did more than the Great Eastern to
induce a brisker state of trade. It not only came out as a real express line, but
opened new markets for fish, vegetables, roots, &c., offered new facilities for the
carriage of manure, sand, bricks, timber, &c., and left no chance untried for
brightening matters.

panies have a quinine of their own. The reason no doubt is that
their executive live in a scheme of constant motion, so that the
gloom around never has a chance of settling down to blur their
enterprise.

So much for the *morale* of our railways; now for the difficulties
of the work performed on them. In England these difficulties are
exceptional, for two reasons. First, the variety of geological
formations to be traversed, and surface inequalities to be overcome; second, the crush of traffic. In no other country is there
such a hard task set before the engineers and the management of a
line.

About 400 expresses * run across England every day, over clay
uplands, underneath our ramparts of chalk, past rosy heaths of
Surrey or muddy "rhines" of Somerset, along levels of hazy fen,
through undulating sandstone of the Midlands, into deep oolite
valleys, up blue limestone dales, over wild Pennine moors of "mill-
"stone-grit," and upon the spongy "mosses" at their foot, amidst
the thick gloom of coal-fields, out again on the edge of the sea,
high up on the empty hills, below among crowded factories, mile
after mile by day or night for a hundred miles on end,† in summer
and winter alike, through fog or storm, at a speed barely less than
that at which nerve-tremors throb in our own bodies.

The passenger, pleased with the pace, is apt to feel as if main
lines were the world and each express an Alexander. He forgets
the endless goods trains, whose drivers frown as he scurries past;
the "urgent" trains of fish or meat, the caravans of coal and
minerals, the flocks and herds removed alive on wheels, the ballast-
trains ubiquitous and casual, the "cheap trip" and costly "special,"
the "light" engines, the pilgrim trolly, the knots of platelayers for
ever toiling at their interrupted task; and over all this a course to
be kept clear through busy station and tangled junction, while the
entire course of the run is meted out with new permission every
mile or two, and is every moment on the verge of being checked.
The traveller never thinks of these and a thousand other items;
but our leading railways have a task to manage as involved as that
of the human circulation.

And yet there is nothing in England more grumbled at than
railways—a fact which may help to explain their efficiency. The
ordinary Englishman having his "genius for administration," and

<hr>

* See note, p. 4.
† King's Cross and Grantham .... 105¼ miles.
   St. Pancras and Leicester................................. 99¼ ,,
   Carlisle and Edinburgh (*viâ* Hawick) .... 98¼ ,,
   Nuneaton to Willesden .... 91¼ ,,
   Preston and Carlisle .... 90 ,,

being more or less also a partner in the business of some railway firm, must find expression for his interest by persistent healthy grumble. Thus, to judge from the tone of contempt evoked when an instance is reported of railway mismanagement, a stranger might suppose that railways were one of our worst institutions, inert and decaying corporations, or that they formed part of that rigid web which encloses industry when "under Government." Instead of which, they are vigorous and free in elastic growth, and the nation is really proud of them.*

But when a great invention like that of railways brings us not only immense advantage but also some concurrent mischief, there are plenty of people who will confine their attention to the latter, and are keener at carping than at appreciating merit.

However, there is no need now to write testimonials in their favour. Of an express we may say, in the words of Messrs. Gilbey, "its value can be proved by comparison," for the hottest advocate of past times would be the first to desert his colours if confronted with the travelling realities of fifty years ago. We have long grown accustomed to the ease with which we can get anything from anywhere in no time, while the doubling of our population and trebling of our trade by means of railways are facts too homely to excite reflection.

Still there is a pleasure in passing through our minds some of the greater reasons why we value this modern gift of speed. It has opened out new worlds in life, and we, like boys of seventeen, are scarcely conscious of the full extent of the change.

1. *New Energy induced.*

The first use of great speed is to heighten men's working energy. This increase comes doubly, first by an access of new intensity, and then by the spread of this through the system so as to augment the amount of force afterwards generated. All fixed capital has this effect, but instruments of locomotion more than any. For when men are tethered, their energy is soon damped by the exhaustion of the local opportunities available, while the farther they can range the more good fortune they may come across, with the greater resultant tonic to their nature. This is specially the case with traders, to whose prospects of sale distance

---

* If an *express* is taken as a train which runs its entire journey, *including stoppages*, at a speed of *forty miles an hour*, then the Great Northern has a daily express mileage equal to that of all the railways in the world outside England. This line is mentioned, not because it runs as many fast trains as the North Western or Midland, but because it runs the most of any in proportion to length or capital.

lends great enchantment; home possibilities are soon counted up and apportioned, but hope belongs to the distant market. And when merchants operate at a distance, speed can work wonders by saving them from that "hope deferred" which eats the marrow out of enterprise. They buy or sell across a continent, and the results face them in a few days.

But the speed of goods trains depends upon that of expresses, and so we are brought to consider the transit of men themselves for business purposes. Here we have a modern change paralleled only by the Bessemer process for the rapid conversion of iron into steel. It is not the mere gift of so much time, for a saving of time and strength is common to all scientific inventions. It is the invigoration put into men's energy by *the quick conversion of intention into deed,* which is the most valuable effect of expresses. By means of them a man's purposes become action all over the land in thousands of cases where formerly no purpose could have been entertained because of the time that must have elapsed before initiation. Now an express takes Purpose white-hot at its origin, whisks it off into warm contact with other living centres, and lights up Action across an area of opportunities. Such swift speed makes one organic whole of the practical ideas scattered here and there, so that the local vigour of the country pervades the whole mass in through currents, which return to revivify the centres of their birth; industrial life becomes intensified as bodily functions are by the establishment of cerebro-spinal nerve tracks among the local "sympathetic" ganglia; there is more and more an *orchestral* effect in life.

High speed enables men to do more work and do it better, to come across a wider choice of facts and form surer decisions for dealing with them. Then the ready response from without to a man's own intention within, this prompt ability for the mobilisation of business ideas, acts upon human nature with the force of a magnet; men feel drawn out to attempt things simply because the plan will at any rate not suffer impediment from distance. And there is a special magic in the transformation of distance from a drawback into a stimulus. A man's nerves are quickened and made more staunch; for such a difficulty being so easily mastered, all others seem less masterful, and realisation appears close at hand. Distance becomes possibility, and the mere knowledge that these possibilities are now within the range of practical dealing makes a perpetual tonic; our imagination has more capital to live upon, and brisk imagination is the spring of enterprise. This is particularly the case where it is a question of combined action, when a coalition is required of distant individuals; because enthusiasm cannot always go by post, but by express it flies like a Promethean spark,

to fuse isolated thoughts into one ardent project.   Men strike while
the iron is hot, and *coelum non consilium mutant* may truly be said
of those for instance who step from their carriages at King's Cross
intent upon the same purpose with which they entered them nine
hours ago at Edinburgh, only braced a little by the splendid dash
across nearly five degrees of latitude.

And this new energy arrives in a further way, by the creation
of a better quality of intelligence.   The constant necessity of
taking up new attitudes towards fresh facts begets an alertness of
mental disposition, a readiness in resource, and a fertility of mind,
which are the welcome trade-winds of the nineteenth century.

Express trains are to a country what long thighs are to an
individual, but long thighs and *intelligence* are said to be related ;
and thus the profusion of English expresses is a happy sign, for
it is the growth of intelligence that gives the world half its
buoyancy.

2. *Pain Lessened.*

A second result, too large for appreciation, is the mitigation of
pain, chiefly in young people.   We have been considering above
the primary use of express trains, how they simultaneously econo-
mise our effort and stimulate us to stronger exertion ; and this is
their common-sense endorsement.   But there is another every day
reason why fast trains have become part of our favourite furniture,
that is, the remembrance of what they do for us in emergencies.
Times of sudden joy and trouble have forged a friendship with
expresses.   When events are urgent, whatever can rise to the
occasion and help us is regarded with affection ; the humming
engine, eager to floor time and space, stands out as something
human, and the guard's whistle trills in unison with our own im-
patience.

Those old pathetic pictures of partings, when some one of a
family left the home in a secluded parish to live in the remoteness
of another, or when a lover was taken from his lass, will not be
painted again, nor will the quiet misery they commemorate have
to be borne again.   This has gone, as the horror has gone which
used to be faced when chloroform was unknown ; the sting has
been taken out of sharp agony, and express-speed has carried off a
pall of dull trouble which clouded many more people.   Nowadays
the softest girl has her cruelest parting soothed by the winged
words that reach her next day through the post, and the warmest-
hearted mother finds that her boy cannot be more than a few
hours' journey from her ; both learn to measure their loss by the

ease with which they may override it. In fact, a dispersun of the
units of a family which used to approach tragedy, is now often
transmuted into an effect of excitement rather than pain. The
penny post has spread sunshine across the world, but the penny
post is only a corollary of express trains, and, comforting as a
certainty of letters is, the arrival of warm flesh and blood throws
them quite into the shade. Expresses consummate the post.

3. *Transfiguration of the Earth and Men.*

In a third way the habit of express speed does us good, by the
dramatic presentation of *ourselves* and *the earth.* Sixty years ago
the world, to most people, was their own parish, and such phrases as
"the enthusiasm of humanity" were unknown, because the feeling
was unknown, while "cosmic emotion" was also an unborn child,
waiting until men could be frequently touched by the expression of
their mother earth, a thing impossible till travel was a commonplace.

Now we see ourselves lifted up as on a stage by means of
express speed, which brings ordinary men and women before us
with a spice of circumstance that adds a flavour to our natural
liking. Just as natural feelings are touched by Shakespeare, till
they are transformed into something large, and his readers carry
off a lasting gift, so during a run across England in a fine express,
our every-day quotation for the human race rises above par. In
both cases we are subject to a process the reverse of vaccination,
for we get the complaint more intensely ever afterwards.

It is this that makes a station, on some rough morning when an
express is about to start, one of the most educating scenes in a
capital. The display of brilliant ability appeals to our imagination,
the great success to our pride, and the solid worth of the thing is
obvious as we watch the passengers hurrying out from the pigeon-
holes where they have laid down their gold. The train is run for
no one in particular, but the programme of each passenger catches
emphasis and glows with the animation of the whole movement.
The brittle old man of eighty, the placid lady with white hair and
serene brow, that invalid carried carefully on his couch, the
hungry schoolboy wild for a punctual departure, with his pretty
young sister of golden thirteen, the full-blown lovelier girl warm
in her corner, the jovial merchant seating himself like a ruddy
bulwark, those police with a handcuffed wretch between them, the
artisan eager for his new billet, the son on leave to bury his mother,
the two old friends with knapsack and pipe keen for their holiday,
the soldier off to a foreign land, the sunburnt sailor steering

straight home at last, and the deep-lined doctor of repute, driving
up just in time, with thoughtful hope on his toughened face—so
many mortals, old and young, unacquainted with each other, but
bound one way for divers reasons, are merged for a time in one
joint experience, like notes in a fine chord where the combined effect
enhances the value of each constituent.   Life is seen as in a
spectrum, vivid with its various hues and shades, and when the
driving-wheels begin to turn, and the white steam pours out, it is
the departure of a human ray of light and heat to energise some
distant spot.   Stations should have large spans and great architec-
ture; they look down hourly on great services to men.

   Then again, a genuine *national* feeling comes to an instructed
traveller by rail, if the journey is long and swift.   The army of
plate-layers intent upon our path, the sleepless—but often only too
sleepy—signalmen, the busy foreman and inspectors, the porters
prompt for a punctual despatch,* the guard scattering sparks of
alertness, the humorous driver unsoured by repeated loss of ideal,
the honest tapper of every wheel—not to mention those who
designed and put together what has to stand the test of relentless
speed; there must be sound men all along our route, and this comes
home strongly to us after an hour or two.

   But it is the Earth herself that is brought before us with most
vivid splendour, in a way which the present generation is the first
to have experienced while children.   The feeling of distance is
almost modern, and is growing up now as a result of running over
immense spaces in the limits of a day.   When "All that are
" desirous to pafs from *London to York,* or from *York to London*"
used to " perform the whole journey in four days (*if God permits*),"†
they went over the same ground as we do now in less than four
hours, and no doubt a greater number of objects caught their eye.
But they slept two or three nights on the way, and sleep seems
(except in the case of lovers) to dislocate the experience of the
current day from that of preceding ones, whereas now the external
world showers its volley of successive impressions upon men whose
mood has not time to tire from London to the northern capital,
whose spirits are as keen at the last mile-mark as at the first.   And
thus the entire series of objects encountered in the run through
nearly three degrees of latitude make one great picture in our
memory, every detail being in almost equally sharp focus: after
many such journeys there begin to dawn on the plane of our con-
ceptions new outlines of the earth.   Distance is *felt* in the nineteenth
century, instead of being assented to by figures or the lapse of
days.

   * At any rate north of the Thames.
   † Advertisement of express service between York and London, April, 1706.

Then this new sense of *Space* soon merges in and helps to swell that modern feeling of *Existence* which draws nourishment from so many sources. And any one who is susceptible to reality, or who has a tendency to fall in love with existence, must be fond of a run by express. Many a modern brain, aching from inward collision, receives an unrivalled tonic from the pleasant broadside of life that plays on our rapid course with such a kind profusion. Blue mountain-ranges dozing in the distant sunshine, the steadfast river rippling near, the bosomed slopes of teeming soil turned up in glossy ridges, the ardent birds, and comfortable cattle, old houses that peep gray from their shelter of trees, where the doves are cooing as we pass, then a sudden vision of crowded roofs and busy smoke across the sky, the shrill applause from children waiting for our speed, the people pacing on the platform whizzing by, the long-drawn aisles between those lines of tracks of coal or iron down which we dash with the roar of a storm, and soft green fields again, where the white clouds are sailing silent above the curtseying wires —at each turn thousands of living instances never cease to salute the audience of our listening eyes. Whirled with a magnificent ease through a panorama of life so generously presented, the worn man feels more than the atmospheric breeze that blows outside; he is strung by an altogether novel touch from the surrounding fact of Existence.

An express cutting sections through the heart of England, its industry and its solitudes, reminds us of some praise bestowed on a poet of old, because of—

> " his touches of things common,
> Till they seem to reach the spheres." *

For these journeys put a rainbow-fringe around our pictures of the Earth and men, till our feeling about both is enlarged into something like love on a wider scale. An Englishman who knows his country well, if he take his seat by the window on a summer day, must admit, as he is hurried along the exquisite dales of the Derbyshire heights,† or drawn with unfaltering pace up the wild ascent of solemn Longdendale,‡ that of such speed we can truly say, it touches nothing that it does not adorn.

The cows graze on in their happy way, the sheep scamper off in a mob, the labourer looks up with unadmiring eye; a moorland

---

* Mrs. Browning on *Euripides.*

† The Midland expresses to Manchester run up to a height of 999 feet near Peak Forest, where they tunnel a fork of the Pennine range.

‡ From Manchester to the top of the Woodhead tunnel, 1,010 feet above sea, is 22 miles of continuous ascent, averaging $\frac{1}{145}$ all the way, only 3 miles of which are easier than $\frac{1}{200}$; there is three-quarters of a mile level on the way, but no other rest. The M. S. & L. expresses mount this with a very off-hand alacrity.

stream falls sparkling close beside the line; soft ferns and foliage
wave above; overhead the clouds move in stately procession; we
are borne with swift noise past the dark air and keen faces of a
factory town, then lifted up on a level with the bare turf of silent
hills; down again on the plain we watch church steeples sailing in
and out the trees, while the sunlight flits with magnificent sweep
among the hollows of the ranges; cowslip scents come in at the
window, and a girl on the bank walks steadily by, regardless of our
roar, for thoughts of something better; these sights of an every-
day world we see as we may see any other time, but we are more
touched by them now. That high speed which bears us so rapidly
from one to the other raises our mental platform, and the commonest
objects appeal to us more, in the same way that mile upon mile of
ordinary field and homestead become a splendid view when looked
at from a mountain-top. The effect then is so great that it is hard
with the words of the plain to describe what we see.

4. *High Art Leaven and Scientific Encouragement, in Express Trains.*

A fourth gift of express speed is the example of "finish" it
offers, a stimulus to encourage people who are deep in the ruts of
common circumstance. Familiarity with any of our great English
lines breeds a disposition similar to that induced by acquaintance
with splendid music or beautiful figures; the observer feels like
Edmund in *King Lear*, that he pants for life and means some good
to do—at any rate longs to do something well. There is a hankering
after excellence inside every one, but it wants occasion to draw it
out, and there is no charge for admission to the sight of an express.
Now an express is the death of mediocrity, or mediocrity will be
the death of it; and hence the quicker the speed of our trains the
healthier* the effect of this demonstration of high art on a world
compelled to so much that is "cheap and nasty." Certain old words,
descriptive of excellence in men and women, are just now disfran-
chised from the public service. But the qualities they were used
to denote are still extant; signs of them stud the rails at every
yard, and each engine is a moving testimony to their persistence.
Stamina, thoroughness, perseverance, are the "water-mark" of our
English lines. And those who bewail "the noble characteristics of
" the coaching days " may find them all again upon the foot-plate;

* And as for *safety*, the safest line is the one which is the best managed, but
the one which runs the most and the fastest expresses is obliged to be the best
managed; thus, those who prefer *slow* trains must yet acknowledge their debt to
expresses.

there stand men with coal-dust on their faces, but diamond qualities beneath.

And besides this leaven of real high art, one of those influences that give aristocratic zest to a life which without them would be stale and *bourgeois*, there is another of close kinship, the feature of scientific encouragement, which is never absent from any first-class product. Such trophies of achievement inspirit the public imagination, for they serve as samples of the astounding successes that can be realised out of ordinary material by means of disciplined thoroughness and common-sense. As both material and common-sense are abundant, while thoroughness can be nursed by every one to some extent, we go away stronger for having seen an express. Those popular legends or doggerel ballads which in Shakespeare's hands became immortal legacies, or the vague suggestions which Beethoven worked out into movements that carry every one captive, these stages are not farther apart than were the Northumberland coal-waggons of a hundred years ago from the masterly fact of to-day, when we see express-engine and bogie-carriages flash across the fields—improved out of all knowledge of their ancestry, were it not for the four-foot nine between their wheels, which still survives as a link of identification with the past.* This brilliant realisation of railway speed, by displaying one instance of our power over the monsters that used to frighten us—for the race was cradled like Hercules—gives intellectual satisfaction and readiness for the next problem. If some difficulties have been so ably mastered, why not others, for they all agree in being difficulties?

Human difficulties always turn out to be difficulties in coping with *material*. The hardest problems set the race are those with which their own physical nature confronts them; and comfort, to say nothing of happiness, will never be known to the greatest number until men take kindly to the study of the way in which lives are conditioned by their own material. When they do, we may look out for gleams of social sunshine. Flesh and blood is surely as amenable to skilful treatment as iron or steel, and quite as disposed to become the subject of a happy transformation. Only some people will talk as if flesh and blood were not material, impressionable, and consequently capable of being modified by skill in any required direction. And the public avoids as long as it is able

---

* 4 feet 9 inches was the gauge of the local coal-carts near Newcastle, which Stephenson adopted as the gauge of his first railway, in order that the coalowners might the more readily fall in with his revolutionary change. [And similarly we may discover certain idiosyncracies of human nature which have persisted till the present day as " survivals;" they may have no merit of their own beyond that of transitory necessity, and we may reconsider their value without alarm.]

any business-like attempt to grapple with the material problems of its *own* nature. It is the natural shrinking from inspection of wounds or a corpse. But, as it is by overcoming a similar repugnance that doctors arise and change disease into health, so, till the public overcome their childlike horror of inspecting social wounds, they will never see the world victorious over the misery which now infests it.

Thus colliery wagons have been in less than a hundred years transformed into express trains, but slums and paupers and filth and wretchedness still abound in the land where these trains most excel. A man who can afford feeling will either smile or be grim when he sees the "Dutchman" charge across the Somerset moors, and then looks over the hedge at the labourer knocking dung about the fields in a god-forsaken automatic way. His "standard of comfort" is inhumanly low, and yet he has the grace to grow humorous on such a life. What then might not be done with such men if the nation would try? They might "suffer a change" into something as "new and strange" as the development of an express out of colliery wagons. But, says the objector, this last was a simple "material" problem, merely a great success in managing materials. There *are* no other *kind* of problems presentable in this world, though some are simpler and some very complicated. Social difficulties, coarse or delicate, the obvious or the subtly pervading, are all alike, as men find when they come against them, difficulties of knowing how to manipulate (human) *material*, so as to persuade a happier result out of its properties and tendencies. Those who succeed in solving these problems must be men of the same kind as those who made railways possible, men who have an instinctive fondness for "stuff,"* and a sympathetic tact in dealing with it.

If then the transformation of gloom and pauperism into decency and comfort is a task differing only in degree, but not in kind, from that of inventing expresses, we should stand upright with hope every morning in London—even in "outcast London"—when the clocks strike ten, and straightway from each point of the compass a brilliant sample of success darts forth on its encouraging career.† The last carriage turns the curve out of sight, but the

---

* "*We are such stuff as dreams are made of.*"

† dep. 10 a.m.	King's Cross	*Scotch* express
	St. Pancras	Fast *Leeds* exp.
	Euston	*Scotch* exp.
	Paddington.........................	*Birmingham* exp.
	Victoria	*Pullman limited* to *Brighton*
	Charing Cross.....................	*Continental* exp.
	Holborn and Victoria	„
	Liverpool St.	*Norwich* exp.

smooth rails remain to look our imagination in the face. They lie like shining clues to guide us on the track of all success, consideration for material. Civilisation will have to condescend to this Jordan before it will be freed from certain leprosies.

5. *The Mind Braced by Straightforward Action.*

We must be grateful to expresses for another healthy influence particularly welcome now. At a time when legislation lingers, or has to fight its way by inches, when the channels of trade are blocked by stakes of ignorance or torpedoes of speculation, when thoughtful people, whether they know it or not, are deadened by that mental pyæmia due to "impacted" problems—then is the time when we turn with thanks to a sight like that of English railways, where every day in a hundred directions, all over the country, wet or fine, peace or war, Tories in or Tories out, we find the same simple *menu* of

"Something attempted, something done."

There is a childish gratification in watching the manly performance of such every-day programmes as those issued by our leading lines; we imbibe a simple medicine which goes straight home, and acts where it is wanted. Those who are familiar with the daily work described in *Bradshaw* derive the same satisfaction that comes to the "gods" of a theatre when they watch the play push on its straightforward march towards the reward of virtue and collapse of the villain; something decisive has been duly done, and they started with the yearning that it should. So in the run of an express there is unity of action to satisfy the simplest. We have to be in a certain latitude and longitude at a certain minute, and start accordingly; we may trust the earth to afford plenty of incident for diversifying the progress of the play. A constant repartee, of hill and tunnel, valley and viaduct, obstacle and curve, a rise or fall in the horizon, *diminuendos* or *crescendos* of speed, uninteresting landscape and fascinating pace, mountain grandeur and a slackening to observe it better, and all the way a dominant strain of one purpose—even when hushed for half an hour at York or Normanton. If we could be only as capable *off* the metals as on, in realising the ends at which we aim.

6. *Individuals coaxed into a Social Attitude.*

The last boon we notice here is indirectly by far the greatest. The primary effect of speed, in augmenting and intensifying the market energy of every man, was manifest with the first train that ran, and this constantly cumulating effect has grown before our eyes, inducing fresh potentiality along scores of secondary channels, till we have the obvious result of it to-day—a nation bristling with eagerness, and intent as it never was before to realise new paths for the discharge of its energy.

The influence at which we now glance works in a rather different way. It does not at first intensify raw local force, for its effect may be the contrary; but it pervades the whole society of individual centres of life, and works a gradual *readjustment* of their attitudes to one another, in such a manner that each unit becomes better disposed to exchange energy with his neighbour. It is this influence which is now to a great extent laying a permanent way for real society, while the first has been breeding a tremendous capacity for working on the new lines when open. When people mix, there is a change as great as when chemical action occurs in a test-tube, but the change is a happier one; the individuals do not disappear, only their characters modify, they become more pliant and more ready to make terms with their fellows, that is, more disposed to create life on a generous scale. As a result of a few years of expresses, we have in England new social phenomena, not simply aggregations of event; while the great British independence or stubborn self-sufficiency of the individual units mixed together has made the result much more valuable.

For express trains are through-currents of life, which arouse localism from its habit of aloofness, and stir up a disposition for contact, for intelligent "society." Then follow through-currents of social enthusiasm, as the linked individuals induce happiness all round, instead of radiating into space. Even now men and women are like bad engines, wasting nearly all their warmth inside them, instead of making it efficient outside; but what were they a hundred years ago? The gradual change of this kind effected by expresses may be compared to the acquisition of respiratory organs; for now the fresh air of intelligence pervades the life of the country, and eliminates the used-up products of clique and custom. Thus the old antithesis of "town" and "country" is fast losing its point, and a modern simplicity* of method is arising which is partly due to the discovery of our greatest common measure by travel. Vulgarity, snobbishness, and parochial servility are dissolving into a thoughtful regard for the circumstances that inclose human affairs. We can see signs of this change all around us—in our books, our servants, our furniture, and nowhere more than in the eyes of children and the dress they wear. Along with this new simplicity may be also seen a new hope, which is coming on quietly

* "Ancient simplicity is one of the illusions that vanish before historical criticism."—F. Pollock, *Fortnightly Review*, October, 1881.

like a sturdy child. Hope arrives in the train of new conditions, and a fresh breeze began to blow over the world when the railway was opened from Stockton to Darlington; for that extra-parochial enterprise ushered in extra-parochial reward.

We might continue dilating on the obvious—for anything healthy has so many endorsements—but a recital of benefactions is apt to fatigue. Before however withdrawing from analytic admiration, we must add a final word in praise of motion. Mill says: "This one operation, of putting things into fit places for "being acted upon by their own internal forces and by those "residing in other natural objects, is all that man does, or can "do, with matter. He only moves one thing to or from another."* And this same operation is all that men "can do" with their fellows. Therefore an express, since its *raison d'être* is the perpetual motion of men themselves, marks the very quintessence of human ability. Now it is about the peculiar

Nursing Effect of Motion

on men thus daily subject to its influence that a word may be said.

Everybody is in love with motion, all living souls are under its spell. Children feel the fascination without asking why, and older people are beginning to understand its power. Each summer they go to the seaside, old or young, for the waves to work their remedy. They have come from places where their lives are stereotyped, where cast-iron custom conditions their ways, where they are down so deep in the ruts of existence that little of the generous sky can be seen; of a sudden they escape from this, and find themselves where there is a lull from routine, where they get up every morning to eat their breakfast with the knowledge that Necessity is miles away, and that their thoughts have a whole holiday. After a few weeks of this new heavens begin to open. Exempt from obligation to do anything in particular, but yet inhaling vigour daily, there comes a readiness for everything in general. Life seems full of possibilities, and its limitations fade away. The vivid sense of power that we receive from healthy traffic in our veins need not now be expended in the usual disbursements of exacting monotony: there are no "first preference" or "debenture" claims to be satisfied here—and so for once Free-will, that poor ordinary shareholder, revels in a dividend.

But most of this magic is the effect of the sea, unconsciously touching the senses all day long. Like the touch of a lover, it

* *Political Economy*, Bk. I, chap. i, § 2.

breeds a quiet superb certainty of power; things *can* be done, and a new effort arises to set about considering *how.* The sea does this by a very simple mechanism. Everlasting *change of motion* takes us in her lap and sings a lullaby. Rocked in this "cradle of the " deep," men soon forget all about particular instances of the year when they came to grief over their task; they only feel their lover Existence—the helper of each particular effort—pulsating close beside them, and this they feel half unaware of what it is. The never-ending waves leap across miles of horizon, while eager Life, undressed by any human habit, Life in its nakedness, looks at us with exhilarating eyes. We ourselves do not think of this at the time—as children do not analyse their nurses—but we are attended to all the same. Then the incessant freshness of foam as the tide comes in, the inexhaustible variety of ripple and roller, the sensitive surface of beautiful water shifting its tints in response to the expression of clouds in the blue above—these little things alone (if anything outside is little) act like a charm.

For novel motion always sets up one effect, Hope in the human heart. Instinct tells that happiness never came from monotonous persistence, that every improvement in the race or individual was owing to some sally out from inertia, some new effort to change conditions, some fresh motion among our circumstances. But are not conditions being greatly changed at each arrival or departure of an express? Each journey represents for every man an effort that would not have been made a century ago, from want of the means to make it. Thousands of these new efforts are occurring every day, till the habit of brisk endeavour has become endemic. The growth of this habit ensures a happier future to the country, because an eager disposition to "try" must do away in time with the most hopeless difficulties.

So that standing on the platform of our great inland stations we watch a salutary stir in the ebb and flow of restless men; we see men under the treatment of Motion, and know there is a chance for them. Over every great railway station—as over a hospital, or indeed at any other scene of engineering operations—the flag of Hope waves bright in the air, while under the roof by day and night our befriending expresses move in and out on their errands of health. In the absence of angels to come and stir our modern pool of Bethesda, we turn a warm welcome to these nineteenth-century substitutes, who condescend not once now and then to break the gloom, but are always with us at work every hour spreading good spirits and encouragement across the land. What the sea does once a year to freshen individual lives the railways are doing every day for the national life, in a manner less picturesque but not less effective.

II.

Having analysed the physiological action of high speed on individuals, we may now wander in a more diffuse examination of one or two of the practical changes it has worked in the everyday life of civilised countries.

To speak briefly, and with apparent paradox, it has made us both stronger and weaker, but the peculiar weakness is itself only possible after the gift of strength. The new strength does not show much on the surface in dramatic deeds, while the new weakness is making men ready for grander things in future. The two changes may be described as a *greater confidence* and a *greater uncertainty.* We will notice them in this order. First then comes the peculiar

Stamina in Modern Hope.

There is an ozone in the nineteenth century air, much of which may be traced to railways. Men are for ever waging war against obstacles, and when a great victory is won over any one of these, the *morale* of the whole army is strengthened; they feel ready now for victory in general. The victory Stephenson* won was over a special obstacle which no one hoped to conquer. His subjugation of distance made a specially vivid appeal to each man's imagination, because hitherto distance had been accepted as the death of so many of the best possibilities. But now Distance was led captive across the land in triumphal procession at forty miles an hour, and everyone saw the sight. While this change was establishing itself the children who were being born took a new view of the material world; they grew up to look upon surrounding conditions as things to be tackled by intelligence rather than as vested interests to be touched with caution. If there were no great

* See pp. 33 and 34.

inventions, the world would soon seem like a cabinet full of intricate grooves and drawers, whose movements can be learnt only from tradition; but any achievement like that of Stephenson makes evident the fact that there are inexhaustible hidden drawers unknown to the old experts, with treasure which can be discovered by any one who brings resolution to the attempt. Every man has a current stock of force to work his daily programme with, but this capital swells or shrinks according as it finds an opening readily or not in the barriers of circumstance. Spirits are "high" or "low" in proportion as each beginning of purpose is too much obstructed or is quickly passed through its working stages. Each block to purpose deadens the energy that forged that purpose, while every favouring response has a magic effect in stimulating fresh creations of the originating effort. And express trains have introduced a new state of things in the world of people's business intentions; men turn over their nerve-capital of purpose ten times oftener than they used, and the result is that they develop a new elasticity of nature, as freshening as the breeze upon a sea-shore. Not only is the practical imagination touched with a tonic, but the raw energy saved leaves so much the more available for higher uses; the working day becomes double its old length, and there is a multiplied intensity to work it with.

But the gain must be immense to men who were once the serfs of distance and who now are free. And this emancipation leads to very much more than its own immediate benefits. Unsympathetic people are never tired of depreciating "those triumphs of *material* " and *mere machinery* " which so illuminate the present century. But the sneer comes from ignorance. None of these things can be done without the partnership of some of the finest moral qualities, and each summit of human excellence resembles all others in being at bottom the result of a victory over inertia. Our devotion to physical science will turn out to have been a schoolmaster which will bring us to a happier social state in the imminent future. And besides, we are beginning to admit now that "common material* " details " are to be treated with respect; they none of them *are* really "common," but are all so "highly connected" that a proper attention to any of them may at any moment result in the introduction of angels unawares. The shadows cast by such angels have been glowing warmer year by year since Hedley, Stephenson, and others spent many a night puzzling over boiler-tubes and the adhesion of smooth wheels.

This then is the insidious boon presented by the sight of our

---

* The same people who talk so contemptuously of "material" progress will say, "Oh, that's immaterial!" when they refer to something unimportant, and thus disclose their belief that whatever is material is important.

Scotch expresses running to Grantham* or Leicester† without a stop; the observer is mentally braced by seeing such a long course of obstacles so simply overcome, and the absence of fetters to such a feat of realisation allows his imagination to stand upright for a moment. The same kind influence comes when we listen to the performance of a great movement of Beethoven. Men walk in, badgered by business friction, or chafed by the fetters of legal delay, and sit down to listen in peace, undisturbed by any earthly jar, while a masterly inspiration makes its unimpeded flight along a permanent way of smooth musical tones to a splendid consummation. Both music and expresses feed the disposition to be enthusiastic, by affording public instances of what can be done when conditions are accurately grappled. The audience go away with a leaven inside them, feeling (though perhaps unconsciously) sure that things in general can be done and difficulties overcome.

Every man had once an infinite programme, but it is never long entertained, because the blocks to particular daily effort degrade his disposition to tussle with remaining difficulties; and *vice versâ* any swift possession of *one* end puts fresh force into his readiness to pursue other ends, makes him revert again to infinite attempt. This illusion of infinite capability, bred by such sights as expresses and such music as Beethoven's, is invaluable for giving men buoyancy. And though it may be an illusion to the men of each generation, it is not a delusion for the race; because human minds are growing, and they feel round corners of the future by anticipation. On the basis of actual sterling work already achieved there rises up an edifice of credit to house the workers, and when they look into their mirrors they see " virtual " images of things to come. The faith of active men springs from their works. Hence railways feed the pluck of their creators, and that instinct of *hopefulness*, which though yet an infant, is full of promise, is one legacy of railway work.

But now for "the poor," who form the bulk of every nation. Till the present century what chance had they of such a feeling as Hope? Unvaried persistence in helplessness could scarcely breed it, accompanied as this was by weekly inculcations of the duty of passivity. To the poor in those days the horizon of their prospects closed in dull around them, and was rarely brightened by any gleam of change. George Eliot says, " In the earlier ages of the " world, we know, it was believed that each territory was inhabited " and ruled by its own divinities, so that a man could cross the " bordering heights and be out of the reach of his native gods, " whose presence was confined to the streams and the groves and

---

* 105½ miles.　　　　　　† 99¼ miles.

" the hills among which he had lived from his birth."* And
Mr. F. Pollock, referring to early times, says, " All local courts had
" their own particular customs. There was no general system of
" administering justice common to the whole country."† Such a
state of things may have been all right for people happily placed,
or for those secure from poverty and misfortune. But for those
who were comfortless, whose " native gods " had left them miserable,
to what others could they apply, in a time when men seemed to be
going out of their depth if they moved from their own parish ?
The poor also, weak with ignorance of an outside, were fastened to
a dreary lot by the tether of poverty or the chain of " settlement "
laws. They could not " cross the bordering heights " beyond which
fresh scenes lay, where new chances might be floating in the air,
and where hope always hovered ; but now intelligence supplies
motives to move, and the heights are surmounted in the twinkling
of an eye at a penny a mile. Instead of the old particular gods
and demons of his own district, each man finds the same *régime*
and one common understanding everywhere, so that the sphere in
which action is plain for him expands accordingly.

Thus now for the poor appear streaks of a sunrise of Hope,
while those who had hope before have a stauncher confidence.

Railways have thrown Men Out of Gear Mentally.

But this modern elasticity of disposition is only one of the
gifts we have received by means of railways; we come now to the
second, which at first sight seems destructive of the other. When
express speed became established as a function of the national life,
a widespread interaction began of the many types of rigid British
individuality, each firmly hedged with the assurance of its own
sufficiency ; there was an interference allowed of currents of energy
hitherto insulated. This mingling has now become so general that
an unprecedented state of things has ensued. The air seems filled
with a precipitate of shapeless beliefs,‡ shifting and wandering like
flakes in a snowstorm, and we hear people asking whether long-

---

* *Silas Marner.*   † *Fortnightly Review*, October, 1881.

‡ " In consecrated earth,
   And on the holy hearth,
     The Lars and Lemures moan with midnight plaint ;
  In urns, and altars round,
  A drear and dying sound
     Affrights the Flamens at their service quaint ;
  And the chill marble seems to sweat,
  While each peculiar power foregoes his wonted seat."
                 Ode to the Nativity.

trusted fundamental principles are really "true," while others buy books to see if life be "worth living." Men who confine themselves to an atmosphere close with their own thoughts can easily show on paper that the prospect is very wretched, but out of doors, rubbing against one another and facing the encouragement of successful work, this dampness of printer's ink soon evaporates again.

In the game of "twirl the trencher" there comes now and then an incident called "twilight," when every child for a few moments is unseated, and chaos reigns supreme. George Stephenson was the unintentional means of calling "twilight" in our English nursery, and so thoroughly has inertia been disturbed that we are not likely to find our seats for some time to come. Or we may regard our island a hundred years ago as fast in the grip of a glacial period of theologic ice, while now, with the advent of more Nature and sunny intelligence, the massive floes begin to melt away. Whatever similes are used, the fact remains that thoughts and beliefs are at present blurred in their outline, vague and indistinct compared with those of our ancestors. Virtue and vice, some people complain, are nowadays fickle as to their features, which—like those of the Cheshire cat—are given to fading out of focus when we interrogate them. It must, however, be their own promptitude in discovering good or bad tendencies, rather than the tendencies themselves, which has suffered change. We are none of us sure exactly where we are; we only know, from undeniable evidence of science, that we are out of our old reckoning; and so the crew go on working the ship in a curious state of discontent,—especially those below in the heat of the engine room.

But this auspicious fog of discontent, it may be said, is surely due to the persevering work of *science*, and railways must not be allowed to play Jacob with the birthright of another. This, however, is the strongest reason for presenting in full the claim of railways to our gratitude. Science of course is the mother of railways, which are only one of her splendid children; and in praising the fact of express speed we are merely paying our tribute to her by a bit of concrete admiration. "Science" is common-sense gone into training, with imagination to steer, and railways are simply an emphatic instance of what common gifts can do when properly used. At the same time it is not arrogant to claim for railways rather than for science the merit of having produced modern discontent. No doubt it is the scientific spirit of corroboration, which, by making us all more accurate, is convicting us of error, and apparently undoing discipline; but facts, like seed, must be sown, and by what except by railroads have the seeds of fertile thought been drilled across the receptive land? By the printing-press, it may be said; but newspapers and books depend on speed, and it is the *machinery* by which great results arrive that we are here examining. Besides, it is not so much the diffusion of books containing new knowledge as the diffusion of living people who entertain this knowledge which works such a change in the world; and personal contact is a startling factor in an age of expresses.*

If then it is granted that railways have *unsettled* us and made us discontented, the next thing is to point out the merit of this service.

A partial illustration is supplied by the instance of a modern pianoforte, and by a consideration of the way in which it is tuned. The tuner tries to observe deference to the recognised relations of "fourths" and "fifths," but finds that if he rigidly persists in tuning by these exact intervals the notes of one octave, he cannot have through communication with the notes of adjoining octaves similarly tuned. He therefore disregards a little the individual claims of each "fourth" and "fifth," making each concede a trifle from its absolute mathematical precision, and he tunes away through a series of slightly flattened intervals. The result is that starting from any note we have a succession of exact "octaves" (indispensable intervals) up and down the keyboard, and a given number of wires is thus able to yield incomparably greater results, results quite superior in kind.

The application of this simile to railways in their effect on modern thought is obvious; the mere habit of swift locomotion has made us *tolerant.* Continual contact with the diverse views of different people whom we cannot help liking has subdued us into thoughtfulness and into cultivating a disposition to "give and "take." *Toleration* is notoriously the key-note of the latter part of this century, and the children of each new generation are more and more educated so as to be disposed for wider harmony with their fellows. When nations resemble a pianoforte in the ease with which great movements of happy intercourse can traverse the entire "social scale," then there will be a beginning of thorough "society," a disposition of units which till now has not been possible except over a fractional range of the human instrument.

It is 1883 years since "a star appeared in the East." With it came the first intimation that such a change might be effected, that men could be better off if they would live by means of one another instead of *on* one another, if they would readjust their relations with their neighbours according to a system of intelligent rather than blind selfishness. But the idea was too far in advance of any practical instrument for its realisation, and it could not dovetail with the ordinary experience of those who listened to its

---

* As Mr. Gladstone well knows.

attraction. The greatest idea has to wait for machinery to carry it out, and it is only sixty years ago that the crucial details of such a mechanism were worked out by the local engineers on the banks of the Tyne. They of course were not concerned with this idea, nearly 1900 years old, of first throwing the world out of local tune in order that it might then be re-tuned on an "equal" system* of universal relations. They were simply in love with their own work, but they gave the world a practical form of exercise for the expression of its energy which is fast tending to the result originally announced, and without which this result could not probably have been attained. Meanwhile, in the patient centuries intervening, "benighted Europe" had succeeded in establishing a basis of material security and a bond of industrial union; so that when expresses came into play with this un-tuning effect of theirs, they could not shake society in its material foundations, but were only able to throw it out of gear mentally. This they have done, and we are in the noise of the tuning. It is a distracting and uncomfortable time, especially to some selfish keys, who thought they were secure in their sanctuary, and much resent the overhauling. For a time nothing can be heard but the jarring of individual notes sternly tested; but the prospect is brighter, for every now and then we catch a hint of some brilliant passage of which the keyboard will in future be capable.

In fact a little reflection on our modern instinct of *toleration* discovers the two great modern facts which we have already described as legacies of Stephenson. *Why* is it that people now are so much more disposed to tolerate than they ever were before? For two reasons. First, because they are tough with a *new hope*, hope which comes from living in an atmosphere of practical ozone; and this hope, true to its breeding, makes them inclined to believe in new possibilities of good; while the scientific spirit—which railways have done everything to diffuse†—persuades them of the intimate connection between all things: "*there is a soul of good in all things* "*evil.*" Secondly—and here we have the untuning effect of railways—men are *not so cocksure* as they used to be with regard to the glib certainties Right and Wrong; wider information has made them more modest. Thus our toleration is only possible through

---

* A certain amount of precision has to be sacrificed by each of the lesser intervals, in order that we may secure a true "octave;" when the tuner distributes this loss, so that each interval makes the same contribution to the main result, he is said to be tuning on a system of *equal temperament.*

† It may seem an absurd want of proportion to pass by with such scanty notice the immense influence of the Evolution theory on the growth of tolerance ; but we are only considering the *mechanism* by which such irresistible forces become efficient.

the contemporaneous growth of that *confidence* and that *uncertainty* both of which we hold must be affiliated on railways.

There is a tale told somewhere of a too fond youth who was once exiled from happiness and sent to the emptiness of a remote hamlet. There every morning he used to walk to where a line of railway ran through the solitude, where he could watch the rails keeping their even course away into distance. When he stood on the bright metals he felt he was on a level with kind friends and happy haunts all over the country, and this feeling brought them nearer with a little warmth of comfort. And sometimes, out of indulgence to a sick fancy, he would put his ear to the metals, so as to catch the resonance from that favourite spot from which he had just been severed.

Now " science " has taken us from some of our oldest friends, but when we are on a railway, though railways were the chief instrument she used to work her end, we feel in compensation that we are more closely linked with our fellow creatures. We cannot stand on any rural platform, or cross the rails that pass through the dreariest fen, without seeming to be for the moment arm-in-arm with our whole country. The shining track stands out as a channel for better human consciousness, and we see a gift of nerves which promise a new order of happiness. We may be lonely out among the stubbles of discredited beliefs, but the hand that performed the operation will probably heal the wound. The mental gloom so prevalent, which is caused by the admixture of so much new truth, is like what chemists call " a precipitate soluble in " excess," which will disappear when brought in contact with more of its cause.

Feudalism and Localism.

Two minor points arrest our attention when we consider railways. One is the death of feudalism, the other the birth of localism. In fact these are only two aspects of the same process, for it is the growth of genuine localism which has killed feudalism, by striking its own roots into the soil on which the latter used to thrive. Railways, which have broken up the iron fetters of the Middle Ages, have been silently creating a better bond of union. Centralisation will soon find much of its old occupation gone in a land of confederate localism. Those who look round England now can see the beginning of this change in that hardy and sensible local instinct which is cropping out everywhere. This is the disposition that finds one place nearly as good as another for energetic men, and it is radically different from the cockney belief which makes a man miserable unless he is " near town." No doubt at first the effect of railways was to strengthen the *prestige* of the metropolis; but now the tables are turned, and vigorous cities have grown up where there were paltry towns before, in a widespread rivalry of independence. London is still by courtesy called the "capital," but the word conveys a false idea. Liverpool, Manchester, and the other towns in the north put it to shame in things that mark intelligence. The huge city has lost some of the properties of a real capital, and is as much like an enlarged liver as it is like a head.

In this new growth of *localism* we see exemplified the proper working of Nemesis. "Here, at Killingworth," says Mr. Smiles, "without the aid of a farthing of Government money, a system "of road locomotion had been in existence since 1814, which was "destined, before many years, to revolutionise the internal com- "munications of England and of the world, but of which the "English public and the English Government as yet knew "nothing."* Hedley made his experiments at Wylam, Stephenson at Killingworth; *Wylam* and *Killingworth*, who knows where these places are, except the immediate natives? It was the plucky local spirit that created railways, and this is the very spirit which is now being daily strengthened and dignified by their influence.

With regard to *feudalism*, and its disappearance before the magic touch of speed, we need only recall those words of Dr. Arnold, uttered forty years ago in a flash of intuition, when he saw the first trains on the North Western on the line near Rugby. "I rejoice to see it," he said, as he stood on one of its arches and watched the train pass on through the distant hedgerows—"I rejoice to see it, and think that feudality is gone " for " ever." That system has had its day, and we will not stop to speak ill of a bridge that carried us over in very rough weather. But, though the feudal system is dead and buried, injustice still remains. And some serious people are talking now of a social revolution which will soon come, when the poorest class will extort by force what "greedy capitalism" is too unjust to concede. Whether, or not, in sensible England any such violent change will occur, and passion prevail over intelligence, it is certain that in the meantime there is actually in operation, every day, a remedial force which is none the less capable because it is quiet in its action. Any one can see that railways are the worst enemies of injustice. For injustice now can hardly lurk in the remotest corner when the "bull's eye" of express communication lights up every parish in the land.

To give one concrete instance : At the beginning of the

* *Lives of the Engineers*, vol. iii, chap. viii.

"nineteenth century" trades-unions were illegal. But now that the plain truth about them is diffused, and their doings brought before every one's eyes instead of being known only by false report, these societies are protected by law as much as the wealthiest interests that used to crush them. Railways have been their good fairy.

And so with the many long-endured facts that disgrace society, though we may not yet have got much beyond a naïve indignation arising from the novelty of our knowledge that there were such evils, still it seems probable that in a very few years this resentment will find expression in some intelligent action for their prevention. It is the railways have excited this indignation, by bringing the evils before us so dramatically, and with such a wholesale shock. Men always knew that injustice and wrong went on within the radius of their own parish bells, but they were accustomed to it from their birth, and too lazy to want to alter it. But now railways bring us news every day with our breakfast that similar injustice constantly occurs in every other parish. We cannot stand this—we must protest against the beam when it protrudes from our brother's eye. Besides, a wrong state of things in one parish made no such vivid impression on our minds as the dramatic presentation of Wrong affecting hundreds of thousands. The consciousness *en bloc* is too strong to be resisted, and inertia has thoroughly waked up.

We can see, then, that railway speed has long been working a "silent and insensible" revolution—to quote the phrase of Adam Smith,* when he speaks of an equally momentous change effected by equally "material" agency. Indignation by itself cannot cure wrong, but the best of railways is, that while creating a widespread sense of wrong about social facts, they simultaneously promote that mingling of men and contagion of thought which are the only source of a remedy. For motion is the favourite soil of intelligence.

---

* *Wealth of Nations*, Bk. iii, chap. iv.

III.

By this time the reader will bring forward the objection that we are depicting Railways as a sort of Holloway's Pill, containing the promise and potency of everything good. Such a reputation, however, is, in the case of railways, genuine, founded on fact. For if the function of express speed is to heighten national life, it thereby supplies the country with better energy to remove the national evils from which it may be suffering: and better energy is the one universal specific. And the *cause* of several phenomena is that circumstance whose removal would be followed by the withdrawal of the phenomena. Now imagine railways suddenly destroyed and the art forgotten: where would be any of the specially modern features of this nineteenth century? In fact, "Nineteenth Century" only means what has happened in the decades coeval with railways..

This assertion may seem less like quackery if we remember how many of the greatest social improvements have been worked out unintentionally. Again and again noble ideas have been clearly conceived, but have never come to much because there was an utter absence of machinery for carrying them out in practice; like Pygmalion with his Galatea, the world has watched them go back again to their pedestal, breathing fascination for a few moments, then beautiful but cold. On the other hand, happy prospects have been established by the unwitting humdrum operation of some every-day mechanism that had its birth in mere love of invention, unaware of Humanity, and guileless of any designs on its future. The ways and means of Nature, when we are taken behind the scenes of history to see the mechanism, show an impartiality that is delicious and a *naïveté* refreshing to contemplate in a caucus age. According to a mood fashionable in some quarters, Governments of the future would not only provide their subjects with daily bread, but would be expected to prescribe motives and cater for the incentives to daily action. Conduct so begotten would hardly exhibit that *variety* which affords Evolution its fulcrum to move the race; and certainly expresses were not bred so. There is a friendly humour about the fact that the *occasion* of an immense change for the better has been often something in itself quite ordinary: it gives us all a chance.

Express speed is—in its social effects—almost equivalent to the acquisition of a new sense; and on looking at the manner in which railways quietly began seventy years ago, we find a fascination more than expresses themselves could create: we seem to catch echoes of similar changes seventy thousand years ago or long before, when the living creatures of the time were now and then raised into beginnings of higher sensibility by the simple operation of some outside occurrence on their every-day energies.

How it was done.

The discovery of America was due to (1) *gold dust* and (2) a *misrepresentation.* The Portuguese "had been endeavouring, during " the course of the fifteenth century, to find out by sea a way to " the countries from which the Moors brought them ivory and " gold-dust across the Desert."[*] In doing this they gradually coasted down Africa till they discovered the Cape of Good Hope, a cape so named because, once round the southern point of Africa, there came a hope of being able by this new route to compete for the precious trade of *India*, which the Venetians, by possession of the Red Sea route, had till then monopolised. But these Portuguese explorers, from motives of vanity and self-interest, partly also from ignorance, represented the distance *via* Cape of Good Hope as much greater than it really was. Columbus therefore, assuming the earth to be round, naturally concluded that the farther it was to India by the east, the nearer it would be by the west. Hence that lonely venture across the Atlantic, and the arrival of the ship at what they christened "West Indies." So unintentional was the discovery of the land they did alight upon, that the name remains to this day as a record of the real object of their search.

The new world introduced by Railways was arrived at quite as accidentally. During the great war with Napoleon I. there was, at *Wylam Colliery*, a little place 9 miles W. of Newcastle, a clever young "viewer" called Hedley. "The Continental *war having* " *increased the cost of horses*[†] *and their food*, Mr. Hedley's attention " was directed to the necessity of obtaining some cheaper mode " of carrying coals from the pit's mouth to the river Tyne at " Lemington, where the coals were transferred to keels. The " 'rail-way' from Wylam Colliery to Lemington was about 5 miles " in length. At first the way was of wood (these wooden ways

---

[*] *Wealth of Nations,* Bk. iv, chap. 7.

[†] These extracts are from a little book by Mr. M. Archer, of Newcastle-on-Tyne, in which the truth of its title, "William Hedley the Inventor of Railway " Locomotion," is thoroughly proved.

" came in during the seventeenth century), worked by the old
" method, one horse drawing one wagon. About the year 1808
" the wooden rails were taken up, and (at the suggestion of
" Mr. Thomas, of Newcastle) cast-iron plate-rails substituted.*
" (The gauge was about 5 feet, the same as the ancient wooden-
" way.) After this alteration the horses took two wagons each,
" but it was found necessary to keep spare horses. . . . . . In 1811,
" oxen were tried and worked for several weeks, being shod with
" iron, but the result was not satisfactory. The year 1812 came.
" Mining labour was high, and colliery materials excessively dear.
" Hedley saw that something must be done to lessen the expenses
" against the colliery, and, as the conveyance of the coals to the
" river was a large part of the expense, his attention was naturally
" directed to economy in that direction. To a man of his energy
" and ability, the idea of the colliery having to be closed was
" painful to contemplate; consequently, the construction of an
" efficient engine to convey the wagons, in place of horses, was the
" subject of his constant thoughts. Trevithick, Blenkinsop, and
" the Chapmans had all tried their utmost to make a workable
" locomotive, such as would supersede horses on colliery wagon-
" ways. But success seemed to be as far off as ever. There were
" many difficulties in the way, and the greatest of all was *the*
" *general idea prevailing* that effectual locomotion must be obtained
" by having some *fulcrum* upon which to operate with steam; hence
" the *rough wheels* of Trevithick, the *rack rail* of Blenkinsop, the
" Chapmans' *chain*, and Brunton's *moveable legs*. . . . . . The owner
" of Wylam Colliery, Mr. Blackett, had already caused a locomo-
" tive to be made on Trevithick's plans, which was quite useless;
" and had applied to Trevithick to make another, when the
" ' viewer ' took the matter into his own hands." To quote the
words of Hedley himself in continuation: "I was, however,
" forcibly impressed with the idea that the weight of an engine
" was sufficient to enable it to draw a train of loaded wagons. To
" determine this important point, I had a carriage constructed with
" four smooth wheels, which were worked by means of cog-wheels
" and four handles, two on each side. The carriage was moved by
" the application of men at the four handles; and, in order that
" the men might not touch the ground, a stage was suspended from
" the carriage itself at each handle for them to stand upon. This
" carriage was placed upon the (Wylam) railroad, and loaded with
" different parcels of iron, the weight of which had previously been
" ascertained: two, four, six, &c., loaded coal-wagons were attached
" to it. I thus ascertained the proportion between the weight of

---

* This however is said to have been done at *Sheffield* as early as 1776.

" the experimental carriage and the coal-wagons at that point
" when the wheels of the carriage would turn round without
" advancing. The weight of the carriage and the number of
" wagons were repeatedly varied, but with the same relative result.
" This experiment was decisive of the fact that the friction of
" the (smooth) wheels of an engine-carriage upon the rails was
" sufficient to enable it to draw a train of loaded coal-wagons.
" An engine was then constructed (in three months and a half),
" and fixed on the carriage; it (had only one fire tube) and went
" badly, the obvious defect being want of steam. Another engine
" was then constructed; the tube containing the fire *was made to*
" *return* again* through the boiler : . . . . . the engine went well;
" (May, 1813) . . . . . it regularly drew eight loaded coal-wagons
" at from 4 to 5 miles an hour, on Wylam railroad, which was in a
" very bad state . . . . For a length of time each new engine went
" better, and took more wagons, than its predecessors." (Hedley's
letter to Dr. Lardner, 1836.)

Hedley had, in fact, as part of his day's work, hit upon the
solution of what may justly be called *the* crucial point about the
locomotive : he had proved that the mere weight of an engine
would cause enough pressure at the points of contact of its wheels
with the rails to supply a fulcrum for the forward movement of a
train many times heavier than itself,—*even when wheels and rails
were both smooth.* That is, on applying steam to the piston and
thence to turn the wheels, so tight would be the adhesion through
gravity of wheels to rails at the points where they touched, that it
would be easier for the wheels to yield by turning forwards (and
dragging the train after them) than by " slipping " round, if the
train to be drawn were of suitable weight. The engine, though
moving itself through space, would, as it ran, with nothing but
smooth rails and the Earth beneath, continually create fixed points
on its own wheels against which its own steam would obtain
resistance sufficient for horizontal movement. Smooth wheels
running along smooth rails would take their fulcrum with them.
Too much praise cannot be given to the man who found this out by
practical experiment,—and his name was William Hedley. He
must have served his apprenticeship with common-sense. For
" the general engineering talent of the country sought other aids to
" locomotion, and, even when the smooth wheel and rail principle

---

* " This flue was oval; the curved part required careful workmanship, and
" some difficulty was experienced in finding anybody to undertake it. Ultimately
" a man named Parker, employed at the Tyne Ironworks, Lemington, undertook
" to make it for the sum of 5*l.*"—(Mark Archer.)
　　Bravo, Parker! this was a good 5*l.* for the world.

" was in actual operation,* its importance was not immediately
" grasped by others than the Wylam people." (*Archer.*)

" As a first effect," Mr. Archer continues, "*this engine*† *probably*
" *saved the colliery*; its after effects we may see all over the world.
" There are many famous dates and famous places, but, if we
" consider the changes effected by locomotives, ... we may
" reasonably ask what date and what place are more worthy of
" fame, than May, 1813, and the old wagon-way from Wylam to
" the Tyne?"

None; when the truth is known. Yet what date and what
place are more utterly unknown to the general public? The
phrase we have italicized above explains why the name of Hedley
never travelled far from the Tyne; and it also exemplifies the
child-like way in which immense changes begin in Nature. Hedley
did not sit down with goodwill aforethought to plan a revolution,
but merely bestowed much hard work on a certain item of his
daily routine which happened to be obtruded on his attention by
the necessities of the moment. Intent on his business of making
the colliery " pay," he made railways possible *en passant*; he gave
to the world what was meant for—Mr. Blackett. This immediate
end of his attained, " Hedley was chiefly occupied in developing
" the Collieries with which he was connected, leaving others to
" reap the advantage of the experiments and discoveries he had
" made in regard to locomotives." (This seems to hint a lack of
imagination and enthusiasm.) Nor was there any dazzling leap of
invention,—*Natura non facit per saltum*; he only moved a Watt
beam-engine on to a smooth-wheeled truck, both well-known

---

* " The first Act obtained for the construction of a railway was that of the
" Surrey Iron Railway Company in 1801, for a railway from Wandsworth to
" Croydon. Then followed the Carmarthenshire, the Kilmarnock and Troon, the
" Severn and Wye, the Berwick and Kelso, the Gloucester and Cheltenham, and
" other small undertakings, with an aggregate of 250 miles, and an authorised
" capital under a million. It is almost unnecessary to add that *animal power only*
" *was contemplated in their working*. The Stockton and Darlington Act was
" obtained in 1821, and, *while animal power was to be relied upon* for working
" the line, the clause in the Act states with men and horses ' or otherwise.' George
" Stephenson was appointed engineer immediately after this Act was obtained,
" and, at his urgent request, Edward Pease applied for a new Act empowering
" the company to work the railway with locomotive engines."—(*Whitaker's
Almanac.*)

Had Hedley's engines been properly known to the public, Mr. Pease would
have applied for this at the first (see p. 32.)

† Known as the " Wylam Dilly," now in South Kensington Museum. It was
at work till 1862, when the colliery was closed.

This engine had the three chief requisites of our express engines: *smooth
wheels*; the *heating-surface increased* by bending the flue back again, an idea of
which the multitubular boiler is only a more efficient but less economical exten-
sion; thirdly, the *exhaust* steam was discharged *up the chimney*, so as to increase
the draught.

objects. His ingenuity lay in seeing how these two could work together for one result, and in the straightforwardness with which he proceeded to combine them. Ingenuity like this shows a graceful directness of mind to which the world owes the *initiative* of many of its greatest improvements.

But campaigns must be *carried out* to maturity as well as initiated: a General must be found to steer the new Idea through the obstacles of inertia, and finally make it a *fait accompli*, a living thing able to grow on its surroundings. "It was Hedley who gave " the locomotive its life and power, and made the work of other " men possible." We will now consider one of these "other " men."

At *Killingworth*, a colliery a few miles north-east of Wylam, the engine-wright at this time was a young man by name George Stephenson, who had a great local reputation for his mastery of mechanism. Jonathan Foster, the engine-wright at Wylam, who was foreman in constructing the engines designed by Hedley, was an intimate friend of Stephenson. By means of this acquaintance Stephenson was able to make frequent visits to Wylam wagon-way, where, much to Hedley's annoyance, he picked up the details of construction in the successful locomotive. Encouraged by the owners of Killingworth, Stephenson set about making a locomotive, but, though he had the advantage of a previous example, his engine, when tried in July, 1814, completely failed. "It was a " poor copy of the original, and it failed in consequence of not " being a complete copy."

"Notwithstanding this failure, Stephenson's experiments pro- " ceeded, and may be said to have continued until 1828 before a " locomotive equal to Hedley's was produced. The owners of " Killingworth Colliery were influential members of the aristocracy, " and their influence caused general attention to be fixed on " Stephenson's experiments, until the Peases,* and other wealthy " men, became interested in his work. Thus it happened that " Hedley was obscured, and the Wylam engines scarcely heard of " beyond the immediate neighbourhood."†

Perhaps, too, Stephenson's employers, being educated men, had more power of imagination, and saw more of the future that must

---

* The good-humouredness of things is shown in the part taken by the Pease family in developing railways. Through them the capital was supplied by which a practical start was made, and it was Stephenson's earnestness that persuaded Mr. Pease, and the enthusiasm of Stephenson came chiefly from the sight of Hedley's engines and from a belief that he could better them, while Hedley's engines were directly caused by the continental war: thus war beguiled a Quaker into benefiting the world (and making his own fortune).

† See Appendix, p. 126.

follow from the new "locomotive;" hence their friends "became
" interested " in this bit of Tyneside ingenuity.

But, making all allowance for aristocratic influence, and with
the strongest desire to set forth Hedley in his true position as the
inventor who made expresses possible, we see no reason for taking
away any of Stephenson's real fame. We do not wish to hoist him
on a vulgar pedestal, or to put tinsel on genuine metal. He was
not merely an inventor, but a man of remarkably comprehensive
mind and enthusiastic purpose, full of enterprise and' resource,
who tried to do everything thoroughly well. His perseverance was
simply indomitable, and thus, though he did not originate locomotives, he rose from the status of a pit-boy until he had grappled
the whole subject of railways, and launched them on the world.
Like his own expresses (for he finished by making capital engines),
he had the power of *keeping on,* and so got over more ground than
anyone else. Faith can move mountains—even the inexorable
ones of British obstinacy—if it is faith of the sort recorded in
Stephenson, who worked his way on through his early ignorance
against the dogmas and sneers of professional criticism,* coming
up fresh like Antaeus from every difficulty that floored him. He
stands before us as a Hercules of common-sense action. This plain
pluck, combined with sterling sense, form a character that cannot
be too highly rated. Stephenson was a man, and a leader of men;
and the world is not likely to forget him.

At the same time justice need not be forgotten either. It took
more than one or even two men to present the world with railway
speed. Besides Hedley and Stephenson a whole army of lesser
inventors worked for years, before we got wheels with one flange,
conical tires, the link-motion, the injector, or the hundred other
improved details of our present locomotive,—to say nothing of the
infinite labour bestowed on the permanent way. But the English
like "stars." And so Wellington stands alone with the glory of
Waterloo, Nelson with that of the Nile, in spite of the fact that
those victories were only won because "every man" there did "his
" duty." Columbus, too, must have had some first or second mate

---

* The pluck that Stephenson showed in fighting the wealthy and determined
opposition to the Liverpool and Manchester Bill is enough to make him memorable.
The unshaken persistence with which he, a man of no education and unknown out
of his own district, maintained his case against the ridicule of recognised engineering authorities, could only have proceeded from deep common-sense insight into
the future.

An anecdote may be amusing here. Mr. Alderson, the leading counsel for the
opposition, after speaking for some hours before the Parliamentary Committee,
finished with the triumphant peroration, " I have now done, Sir, with Chat Moss,
" *and there I leave this railroad !*" There it is still, and twice every hour an
express skims across it at a mile a minute.

to whom we owe our thanks, for otherwise the doubting crew
would have turned the vessel back again.

Still, statues take up room, and most men who have done
good work must die without them. But a stranger stepping out
from the busy station at Newcastle-on-Tyne, when he sees the
admirable statue of George Stephenson so appropriately placed,
attentive to the noise of traffic as it comes along his own High
Level through his native air, when he is told, too, that this same
bank of the river, a few miles away, was the birth-place, the
laboratory, and then the resting-place of that man who struck the
first light for Stephenson, even a stranger will feel that this
sculpture would be a finer local monument if the opening of the
tale were recorded there as well.* Perhaps some day in the better
times coming, when the winter wind of competition has ceased to
blow with such a bitter edge, and the spring air of kindness opens
human flowers, then perhaps our heroes will be commemorated in
groups instead of in solitary figures, and then we may see Hedley
standing beside Stephenson,—a double object of affection to every
Tyneside man.

Nemesis.

It thus appears that railways came as it were by accident (in
"a nation of mechanical engineers"). A great wave of commo-
tion on the Continent made in its spread a little eddy at obscure
Wylam on the Tyne, where it stirred up energy which might
otherwise have remained obscure. Like Orlando in *As You Like
It*, Hedley and Stephenson, in wrestling with the high price of
horses and corn, overthrew more than their enemies, and a
Rosalind was won for the world.

But such accidents, though few and far between, must be often
on the verge of happening in many parts of England.

"Where loaded guns lie sparks may make the air resound."

Where fine men and women abound, Nature is ready too, and any
day may see new gifts emerge, like crystals suddenly become
visible. Now the power to start a new idea may be an inheritance
from the male side; but the disposition to steady endeavour for a

---

* " The locomotive did not spring full-born from Stephenson's brain. Hedley
" was the forerunner of Stephenson, and made his success possible. Let us give to
" each the honour that is due to him."—(*Manchester Guardian*, 6th June, 1882.)

A step in this direction might be made if the North Eastern would admit one
of Hedley's earliest engines to a place on the High Level, where Stephenson's
Killingworth engine now stands alone.

distant end, patience to persist unbaffled through a fog of ignorance, stupidity, and long delays, the calm intuition to see what is possible, and common-sense to stick to the statement of it against hysteric opponents, deftness in resource or plan, and that careful devotion to detail which alone can bring forth excellent workmanship,— these things are not found prominent except in men who have had genuine girls for their mothers. And if these qualities were common, the world would soon be cleared of its worst troubles.

So that express speed stands out as a prize for the encouragement of every natural girl; nothing so full of stimulus is offered her by those who canvass for her " Higher education." Whatever else they do, mothers of heroes have to pass Nature's *vivâ voce*.

But returning to Nemesis. As Stephenson succeeded chiefly through his perseverance and intuitive common-sense, we may say that railways owe their existence to *womanly* qualities, that is, to qualities which no man would possess in eminent degree unless he had had a real concrete girl for his mother. Now, since railways have been made, their daily operation has—amongst other things— caused the growth of a very strong instinct to do something for the other sex, a feeling indeed of which the " Higher education " movement is only one manifestation. · More freedom is allowed them in their every-day habits, their disposition is given a chance of developing after its own nature instead of being clipped according to a set pattern, they are more healthily dressed and managed, they travel like boys, and like boys they are considered worthy of an expensive education,—even to a ratepayer a girl is now a subject for dignified thought, and must soon become an object of dignity herself. It is not an exaggeration to say that fifteen centuries of established Christianity did not do so much for women in the way of larger life and happiness as will result from this modern awakening caused by the railway influences of fifty years. It is hardly necessary to point to the altered treatment of " outcast " women " which is spreading every year with decent people. Christian authorities gave a helpless shudder at that fact, but now social intelligence—produced by constant moving to and fro among each other—*tries to improve it*. Much as has been said about Resentment and its conquest by Christianity, common-sense does ten times more to make that spirit obsolete : and railways are the great manufactory of common-sense in social matters. As to marriage, again, when the world hit upon that settlement of an old question, adopting it "for better or worse," no one doubted there was a great deal of "worse" in it. But it is only of late that the suggestion that even marriage might be improved has found a voice or been endorsed by practical advocacy. The Married Women's Property Act, the liberty for women to become doctors, the opening of new occupations for them to earn a living at, and their admittance to a share in municipal functions, whatever the effect of these may be, all serve as straws to show which way the wind of feeling blows. Everyone sees that marriage means a certain amount of "exploitation" of one sex by the other, and that, from the nature of things, the women must generally be the ones who are most exploited. This is the fault of Nature,* and cannot be removed by Act of Parliament: but on that very account we should do our best, by Act of Parliament or otherwise, to prevent anyone from having the chance of superadding to that natural despotism the unhappier exploitation† which a selfish man so easily drifts into through the help of English privacy, custom, and public inertia. Both these sorts of exploitation are as old as Adam, and have been subjects for immemorial cheery jest; but only of late has one of them come to be regarded as a preventible accident, and hence made matter of public complaint. People do not mind complaining of an arrangement when they believe it may be bettered,‡ and hope is now so brisk that it penetrates the retreat of this garden of Eden. Nothing much may have been done as yet—for even railway influences are not instantaneous in their effect,—but if the feeling is there the rest is sure to follow. " When the Ideal has once alighted,§ when it has looked forth " from the windows with ever so passing a glance upon the Earth, " then we may go in to supper, you and I, and take our ease,—the " rest will be seen to."|| Therefore, in those apparently flippant views of adults about marriage which some people quote as signs of the " terribly *unsettling* influences " of the age, others see merely good evidence of a modern manly indignation—part of the general discontent—which promises new happiness to every girl in the future.

If this is so, then, looking back to where railways first began, travellers familiar with Tyneside faces will understand how—after seventy years—railways are only repaying an original debt. But the gift returns a hundredfold: originally due to straightforwardness of nature in some girls of Northumbria, it comes back on women everywhere. Nature is fond of such Nemesis.

* " That strange art which comes so naturally to a woman, of obliterating " herself and her own sensations." (Mrs. Oliphant in "Madam," *Longman's Magazine*, January, 1884.

† " This master, who demanded absolute devotion, and the submission of all " his wife's wishes and faculties to his."—(Ibid.)

‡ " Her calm was the resignation of long usage, the sense that it was beyond " remedy, that the only thing she could do was to endure."—(Ibid.)

§ An Ideal is alighting on the horizon of marriage,—of some one happier than the present average wife, much 'gone off' and spread at the waist, who has exchanged her fresh individuality for a long record of patient automatic altruism.

|| *Towards Democracy*, p. 49.

IV.

*Towards Democracy.**

Everything we have so far examined converges to this. "Democracy" means a new treatment of men by each other, arising from the growth of a new feeling about themselves. It is the outward expression of an inward emotional mood, which makes them long to try fresh behaviour towards their human surroundings. The more items we can be friends with, the happier and stronger we are. But till recently life has been a hole-and-corner affair. The individuals of a nation mixed only in isolated groups; there was little through intercourse. The nation was not organic, but parts of it were separate organisms, feebler for the separation. Two things alone did much for the cause of human nature, Field Sports and the good old parson, for they were at work every day; and these two kept the world together. But the men and women composing it were tied by traditions, bound by prejudice, cramped by "social" (or anti-social) restraints, fettered by fashion, timidity, vulgarity; while over most of the land lay a mist of ignorance as dark as the material pall of smoke by which it is now replaced. Those things are not removed, but railways are removing them. The mere mingling on an open field ensures a contest between better and worse, with survival of the fittest. But the *constructive* effect is even greater: as a locomotive was made by moving a beam-engine on to an ordinary carriage, so when ordinary people of one locality move to another, new kinds of human thought and action suddenly appear.

Theories of Democracy were useless prior to railways. When people came across none but their own neighbours, and each hundredth part of a country was ignorant of how the other ninety-

---

* *Towards Democracy* (John Heywood, Manchester, 2*s.* 6*d.*), a book impossible to have been written before railways,—and a brilliant example of the "modern discontent" produced by them.

nine parts lived, the preaching of new schemes of comprehensive
human behaviour was as futile as a lecture on swimming to boys who
could not enter the water and practise adaptation to its properties.
For fifty years, however, people of every sort and variety have come
across each other, and been intimately mixed up in the affairs of
life. This constant rubbing against one another has taught them
more of the quality of the stuff of which they are all made, it has
caused them to be more kindly disposed to all sorts and conditions
(*wages* have been helped to rise by this change in public disposition),
and while it has in consequence created a wish to level everyone up
to those best possibilities of which his human composition renders
him capable, the incessant contact of ideas has bred feasible plans
for the wiser treatment of that stuff of which high and low are
only variations. This is Democracy, and this is the work of
railways.

Standing anywhere on an English line, the metals beneath our
feet make an almost level path to every town in the land; no
matter how the superficial aspect of the country is, a contrast of
valley and hill, river and mountain-range, we bridge the gaps,
pierce the barriers, and get over the watersheds with practicable
gradients. The ups and downs of Nature thus reduced by the
touch of skill seem hardly the same again; a unity runs through
all the diversities of surface, and we grasp the whole country in
one great picture. This is a simile of the deeper influence of
railways. The intercourse between man and man will soon show an
alteration like that of traffic between town and town. Of a smaller
and smaller number each year will it soon be possible to say that
their birth finds them at the foot of insurmountable hills, or cut off
by gaping ravines from the open country of Life. Education is
laying level spans across those gaps, and public opinion is readier
every day to help in making tracks with easy gradients up the old
watersheds of class-distinction. So that by the time the nation has
ceased to be a deliberate manufacturer of thieves and paupers in
each of its big cities (and workhouses), and when it is ashamed of
the existence of hereditary helplessness against crime or disease,
then we may hope that every boy and girl in England will find
themselves born with steam enough inside and grip enough on the
rails to start on their journey towards higher levels.

Judged by the intervening tragedies, it is a very long time
ago since

> " It was the winter wild,
>   While the heaven-born Child
>   All meanly wrapt in the rude manger lies;"

and since in that old Asiatic world

" The shepherds on the lawn,
  Or e'er the point of dawn,
    Sat simply chatting in a rustic row :
Full little thought they then
That the mighty Pan
    Was kindly come to live with them below :
Perhaps their loves, or else their sheep,
Was all that did their silly thoughts so busy keep."

Had they known that the great Idea of human-kindness was now to be introduced with dramatic force, they might have been sadder men. For looking forward a few years they would naturally have exclaimed with the poet,—

    " Yea, truth and justice then
    Will down return to men ;"

but they would have died without seeing these any nearer. For

    " . . . . . wisest Fate says No,
    This must not yet be so ! "

because it *could* not yet be so. The new idea—new to all except lonely thinkers—was indeed shortly afterwards explained more vividly, and the new lesson taught more earnestly, than is ever likely to occur again. But it could not possibly receive practical application on any public scale. The "brotherhood of man"—their community of descent—was a fact 2,000 years ago as much as now, and "goodwill" was as much an every-day product of human hearts. But the disposition *could not find exercise* as a part of public polity because *the material adjuncts were wanting.* The Roman Empire, the crown of civilisation, was only an immense exploitation ; it fed *on* the nations subject to its rule, and thus destroyed its own roots. Energy saw no way of making progress but by enslaving rival energy—a method as short-sighted as that of living on one's capital. The western world had in fact not yet found out that *by work* a number of nations might prosper together, —a discovery left for the Middle Ages. Hence, as Christianity came out just when this principle of political cannibalism was firmly established, it could not make much way at first. The Roman rule, however, by the uniformity of its administration over such a wide area, served as a sort of "permanent way" for the easy diffusion of the Christian idea ; it was scattered to and fro across civilisation, where it quietly took rest in private hearts, leavening the race until application of the idea was possible.

During the "Dark Ages" that followed the collapse of Rome, the first gleams of modern light were being struck out by the hardy "Gentiles" left to their own devices. A *mechanism* was being gradually constructed by which men would touch each other at so many points and be so closely connected, that the "brotherhood" idea could find free play, and "goodwill" have instruments to work with. This mechanism was the machinery of *commerce*, which slowly made men friends of each other in order to befriend themselves. The pursuit of handicrafts or adventurous trade came to be set up as honest ends for a freeman. Society passed through a long manipulation, by the feudal system, the Church, the trade guilds, leagues, and monopolies, but all this time individuals were becoming more one body, as the old blind selfishness gently modulated into the intelligent variety. Our own century is brilliant with inventions, yet these Dark Ages were the time of the greatest, for it was then the world found out in *confederate work* a method of prospering as superior to the previous predatory *régime* as steam-power to water power. On men thus firmly held together by external ties the invention of the printing-press came opportunely; and stirring thoughts were diffused like a ferment through a society which they could not now dissolve, but only stimulate. Still, the movement of *men* to and fro among others of their kind is the real Promethean spark that warms the world (on this account the Crusades are immortal),—and so the plot proceeds to Wylam-on-Tyne, in the year 1813. Since that date what used to be called the Christian idea has at last prepared to step down into life: human good will is spreading, not by inculcation, but by the sunnier effect of human intercourse; we come across people in travel or visits who are not entangled in our private lives, whom therefore we accost straightforwardly, free from all prejudice,—and we cannot help admiring human nature thus impartially presented. This new natural affection for our kind is not a feeble sentiment; it is already at the bottom of the rough attempts that are being made to replace by something better those antique principles which control and spoil the relations of employer to employed.

So the work begun 1,900 years ago has in the last fifty years received a striking impetus. The invention by Hedley of the first successful locomotive was itself a step in the *process* of the world's advance no more startling or abrupt than the firing of that last fuse which—after years of hidden work—made a communication between the two headings of the St. Gothard tunnel: only in each case the ensuing *change* was abrupt, for fresh air was let in, and a fresh vista lay open for human endeavour. The attitude of mind which used to be known as Christian is now more frequent than before, but in the course of centuries it has acquired new vigour, it is getting naturalized and at home with its surroundings, and we speak of it now as *Democracy.*

Here we must take a momentary glance at

Railways and the Evolution Theory.

What distinguishes the most serious modern thought, and consequent plans for ordering life, from the methods and thought of ancient times?

Formerly all continued high thought seemed to land one in negative apathy. Men must take things as they were, and make the best of them by indifference. This stagnation was caused by the fact that the whole course (if it could be called " course ") of the universe looked like a stagnant lake, or perhaps a swirling pool, in which the same straws came round again and again, a recurring-decimal of good and evil figures. Happiness was to them a fixed amount, drifting about, and insufficient for all; therefore, if any one man did not come across it, never mind; after all, what *is* happiness but an accidental waif? They saw (compared with us) no pathways from the actual to the possible; no roads had been laid down by science, and there were no tracks for energy to work upon.

The difference is tremendous now. There is no such sentiment that we are in a water-logged eddy. Life is felt to be capital, out of which there is no knowing what may not be made. The happiness attainable is, like wages, only limited to a fixed quantity on condition that human effort and intelligence remain what they are. With new effort inspired by the enthusiasm of reasoned Hope, possibilities indefinitely great are to be realized in time.

This sound hope comes from the tonic instilled by the Evolution news, which is really a tale of unlimited improvement. As we begin to be aware of the past, we put reliance on the future. We did not know, out alone on our wide ocean, how far we had moved: science dropped a line overboard, and has begun to read off unsuspected speed. With this modern discovery our encouragement comes from behind,—and therefore all scientific eyes are turned to our traces in the past. The new knowledge has burst on us with a shock of invigoration; there is a renaissance of credit in the universe, and men attempt things they never did before.

How did we get this news? There was hard work, of course, but hard work alone was not the occasion. The " Origin of Species " is a book of immense labour for one man to have written, and one man could not have done it had there not been railways and the penny post, which saved his energy by bringing notice of facts before him instead of his having to go to them. Without railways the facts could never have poured in on a scale profuse enough to support the theory to the satisfaction of Mr. Darwin, nor would the book when written have been launched on the world quickly enough to make a new emotion. The human mind had been tending to the expression of this new idea once or twice before; but just as an unusually large supply of food is said to be one of the most potent causes of a new variation in a plant,* so the advent of railways, by showering in upon the human mind a sudden abundance of fresh facts to feed upon, enabled it to strike out the idea better than any of its predecessors.†

The real Democratic spirit is thus doubly indebted to railways. It derives its *warmth* from the natural operation of that intercourse which railways have made possible, and this raw feeling is *enlightened* by the wonderful illumination thrown over it from the theory of Evolution,—for if the theory is true, the only natural disposition is Democracy. It was a great thing for a man to have said (if he meant it) 2,000 years ago,

" Humani nihil a me alienum puto ;"

but we can go a little farther and express it thus :—" we are all " men, and, knowing something now of the stuff we are, we believe " that the highest human flights are such that not one of us stands " really apart from the ability to learn them." For

" thin partitions do divide
the bounds where good and ill reside :"‡

and however far apart we choose to represent virtue and vice, science shows that human nature has " through carriages " from one to the other. Where this belief is acted on Democracy begins; and it is no new thing in individual cases. Servants have been attached to their masters, and cowards have made brilliant charges in battle, because they were drawn by the magic touch of this disposition. A fine example has scarcely any power of itself, but when it also radiates with human-kindliness in every word and

---

* " It is a rule invariably with us, when we desire to keep *a true stock* of any " one kind of seed, to grow it on poor land without dung; but when we grow for " quantity, we act contrary, and sometimes have dearly to repent of it."—(Messrs. Hardy and Son, Maldon; quoted by Darwin in *Plants and Animals under Domestication.*)

† The same remark applies to Mr. Herbert Spencer, but his statement of Evolution, though earlier issued, is not so known to the English public.

‡ Burns, " Verses to my Bed."

look, the effect is magnetic: humdrum souls feel avenues open
between the ground they stand upon and that they admire above
them, paths which for the moment (such is the power of a word or
look) seem all of possible gradients right through from one to the
other. In this warm flesh-and-blood manner the truth of Evolution
has often cropped out here and there, by the mere instinctive working of healthy hearts; and now that the light of fuller information
is on us, the news should touch men into a general voluntary
adoption of the same attitude.

But what we are wishing to lay stress upon is the fact that
railways have given enlightenment as well as warmth to the cause
of kindness: warmth, by the inevitable effects that accompany
incessant human intercourse, and *light*, by the share they took in
helping to produce the Evolution theory.

V.

Seeing the part she has taken in the play, we must now call

Mechanism

before the curtain, to receive our farewell thanks. She comes
"orb'd in a rainbow," an old friend in a new face, smiling across
the footlights of Intelligence.

The age is one of mechanism and applied science. The noise of
machinery, some say, is so for ever buzzing in our ears that the
music of the spheres is lost. Is it, or are our workshops only an
echo of that music? Why distrust our own age? can we not
catch a kindred "subject" in this nineteenth century variation?

Inside us and outside us, in the minutest microscopic specks and
away in the huge stellar spaces, where is there not mechanism?
What is left if we ignore it?

When there is no corner in England without the whirl and

clamour of machinery, when our eyes and ears are never free from
it, it is only because men have turned themselves inside out, have
found how to make things after their own nature to help them,—
inferior similes of themselves. Why not bear with the discomforts
attendant on a change when we see in it signs of the world learning
a great lesson ?

Machinery is action towards an end, an arrangement of ordinary
items so as to get something definite out of their motions; by
altering the relations of position of ordinary forces we get extraordinary (*i.e.*, for our purposes "better") results. When motion
is gathered together and put through its steps, the resulting dance
we call "machinery." The eternal stir of raw fact and atoms
going on all round us is beguiled through a wonderful *discipline*,
and by this "mechanical" process there emerge in time a variety of
"living" facts or "things." Original tendencies, blind and self-
willed in their impetus, come to *work together* for good : thus a
universe in which once there was nothing but the momentary,
where existence was separate as a waste of sand, comes by degrees
to be one in which countless worlds revolve through orderly space,
where the moon makes a broadening pathway on her silvery tide,
where frost and rain and wind and sunshine discipline the earth
until by their help "plants" and "animals" are established as
successful facts; and after longer discipline again there comes an
age when

> "Life found itself human, and wond'ring, awoke."

Then in time we have lovers to walk in the lanes, and as we listen
to their talk,—

> "The moon shines bright : in such a night as this,
>   When the sweet wind ......"

we cannot help thinking with amazement of the immemorial moonlight nights during which that mechanism—as gentle as it is
immense—must have been faithfully at work before these two
emerged into the foreground of the picture. *Ars longa, vita brevis :*
existence is old, and the art that transforms it into Life works on
for patient ages before it can produce a "human life" that will
last a few years.

"We" are only transformations,—manufactured of what comes
from the sun. Heat and frost and rain undertake the earlier stages
of the process; the plants and animals carry it farther; and we
embody all their help each day to maintain our output of the
finished article. Of all things in the world *Consciousness* is the

most highly manufactured,—worked up with such a finish that we forget there is any raw material. People who sniff in a maudlin way at "mere mechanism" and a "reign of machines" do not know what they are whining at. If our bodies were only transparent, so that we might see—unscared by associations of Death or wounds—the marvellous maze of exquisite motion busy inside this factory, then even men who find the Atlantic "dull," or Niagara "coarse" would send in their adhesion to praise of *this* scene of mechanical art. Everyone would be taken aback at the infinite variety of machinery so admirably arranged which works day and night to produce that article apparently so simple in itself,—consciousness.

It is only because as a rule the machinery works so well that it is not noticed. But even in health, as soon as people cease to vegetate, and come across each other, a new stir runs through the wheels of the mechanism; and, as a consequence, in the final product streaks of admiration, anger, love, or contempt, are superposed on the normal placid pattern of organic life. Disease of the common sorts, when this pattern is torn in holes or pulled awry, and insanity, when the texture is strangely altered,—these speak in penetrating tones of the fact of machinery. We need not go so far as these, however; we shall find food for respectful thought in the remembrance that specks of dust in the eye cause us "pain," and that similar specks floating high in the air cause admiration and pleasure which last long after the sunset glories they occasioned have passed away: if grains of dust can thus promenade the gamut of our feelings, how delicate is the mechanism by which consciousness is created.

When we look at a sunset, or listen to a strain of Schubert, or "fall in love at first sight," the feelings we experience are certainly instantaneous in their occurrence; but that is because the machinery that manufactures them is so exquisitely impressionable, and moves with so little friction. Sometimes we find men who have no eye for a sunset, no ear for music, and are not touched by loveliness so much as by lucre. This shows the machinery must be different in the different cases,—some wheels not there, or out of gear. The Greeks, too, it is said, were not so moved by "scenery" or by children as the modern European is: these facts had not quite the same machinery to impinge upon; for the human organism has received additions by the discipline it has undergone during centuries of Christianity, hard work, new knowledge, and travel. Hence, though the landscape is the same raw material as 2,000 years ago, we, being slightly different machinery, make a better thing out of it.

Consciousness then is not haphazard, and does not come without

D 2

infinite art. If it did, what would there be to impress us in the
most beautiful sights or other splendid feelings? It is knowing
this that Shakespeare says :—

> " With *more than admiration* he admired
>   Her azure veins, her alabaster skin,
>   Her coral lips, her snow-white dimpled chin :"

for it was the fact of living moving *mechanism* that held him bound ;
he was touching the pulse of Nature's method. So another young
enthusiast speaks of " the *white wonder* of dear Juliet's hand." The
" wonder " was that this little bit of white mortal stuff could be the
means of so ennobling him with " love ;" *how* was it done? And
the mere sight of a girl's breathing runs a little respect through the
admiration of the man who sits next to it. For in the case of a
girl we seem to be more taken into the secret; the mechanism is
more frankly disclosed, and men feel a rudimentary awe before such
splendid workmanship. Only fools could even think they despise
" machinery ;" no one *does* despise it,—for what is the worship of
" good form " but a desire to adopt the results of good internal
mechanism if the devotees cannot themselves beget them? We are
all machinery, at least all who *do* anything: and even " dreams "
are the product of a mechanism some of whose parts are not in
work.

   Now just as tiny material details when arranged make the
mechanism of each man's body, so more obvious movements of
machinery are the material requisites for a living *society*. As these
mechanical aids become more and more engrained with the every-
day life of the individuals of a nation, that life improves : new
connections are made between the insulated units, new nerves to
make possible some *national* life ;—and then a new product appears,
a national consciousness, an *orchestra* of lives, composed of the
consciousness of individuals, yet raising these above what they
were before. This may easily sound foolish talk, but we turn for
illustration to any theatre. When before a large audience a skilful
actor appeals to some natural feeling, every man there who is moved
is moved to a greater emotion (if the thing is naturally done) than
if he were by himself; because each spectator is lifted on a conjoint
wave of feeling which simultaneously has its beginnings in each and
then returns entire through the mass of originators. Each feels for
himself and by proxy too. Now " national " consciousness (we
need not anticipate farther) is this sort of a thing on a wider scale
and in a gentler method. Newspapers and books, the wires that
thread the air of every hamlet, our steamers and express trains,
these can all be seen, and these are some of the ever-improving

appliances by which such waves of public happiness will be more
and more created.

> " How sweet the moonlight sleeps upon this bank !
> Here will we sit, and let the sounds of music
> Creep in our ears ; soft stillness and the night
> Become the touches of sweet harmony.
> Sit, Jessica.   Look how the floor of heaven
> Is thick inlaid with patines of bright gold.
> There's not the smallest orb which thou behold'st
> *But in his motion like an angel sings,*
> Still quiring to the young-eyed cherubims :
> *Such harmony is in immortal souls."*

When Lorenzo and Jessica that night in the grounds of Portia's
house asked for the music to be brought outside in the open air, we
can understand why the soft strains carried their thoughts instantly
out to the stars, and then back to themselves.   The same mechanism
runs through ourselves, the " orb," the " stillness," and the " bank "
on which the lovers sat : no wonder they felt at home, one note in
the surrounding chord.

A sudden change of light plays over the features of Mechanism,
and, looking again, we see the face of

Music

where she stood.   " In sweet music is such art,"—Art such as made
the world.   That is why it moves us so ; no other art so simply tells
the method of the universe; listening to it we are hand in hand
and face to face with the secret of ourselves.   But in what art
more than music does mechanism (of the exactest sort) confront us ?
it is steeped in it.   And because it is we have results that entrance
the related mortal : ordinary vibrations struck from common wires
by skill of arrangement form chords and passages which, like living
things, speak out and take the listener captive.   Each melody and
chord appeals to him with an echo of early days and the strain of
existence : he, too, a living thing, is a composition, built up of
ordinary vibrations (into " subjects " only half worked out) ; and
when the sounds of music " creep in our ears " we catch a reminder
—faint but compressed—of all previous tales on this earth : the
keynote of our origin is struck.

To produce this wonderful effect it is true that human skill and
human ears must be called in.   But what is the " skill " of a
composer ? it is born, not made, says the objector.   Yes, but it was
made first, as we are all made before we are born.   And what are
" auditory nerves ? "   Did they always exist, or have they too been

done by Art? Both nerves and skill are the product of that one Art which we are now considering, the untiring art around us.

For the world is music always going on, since it is the creation of beautiful effects out of ordinary ones. To hear this world-music no delicate ears are needed,—only the mental ones of a little honesty, observation, and thought. But the world, we know, is mechanism. So music and Mechanism are inseparable, one fact, and where there is mechanism there is music, if we knew it. If we prefer Mechanism under the guise of Music, let us take it so; like pills in jam, some facts are best disguised.

And why then do we object to mechanism, while we love music? The answer would want a book to itself. Real music is more than what we hear at concerts; that is only one branch of the Mother-Art that fills every nook and cranny of existence. But our musicians, in the sheltered calm of their own thoughts, construct their beautiful subjects, work out their fine ideas, in a few months or years, having no external obstacles to fight their way against; while out in the common universe, where ideas strive in rivalry, it takes ages to realize them as living facts. Therefore the "creations" of our musicians come fresh like fragrance on a fevered brow: men are told for a moment what Life *may* be, when its underlying art has freer play; and they emerge again into the actual every-day world—of block-signals mostly against us—less inert than before, livelier, fresher. For "freshness" is the gift of keeping true to the spirit of Nature, always "trying," like the pulse in our own arteries. Art is fresh, because art is Effort, and where no "art" is there is "inertia."

Does the universe really *like* work? though everything everywhere is ever at work, is work against the grain of things? Art is natural, for Nature consists of art; but is inertia more natural? If so, we can excuse ourselves for behaving rudely to Mechanism. "All work and no play makes Jack a dull boy," and life is a long drill—except for half-holidays of Love—until the vacation of Death is due. Mechanism is the schoolmaster who has brought us on to consciousness, the ladder that has lifted us out of the darker ages of Time, the surgeon who has performed saving operations upon us: but children bear a grudge against the doctor, men who have risen kick away memories of the steps that made the rise tedious, and sometimes boys feel stiff in the presence of their schoolmasters. We like *results*, but hate the processes by which alone they come: the universe yearns to express itself, but soon gets tired of the yoke of discipline under which it must pass to find full expression at the distant end.

Perhaps some of those who most dislike the idea of "mechanism" are those who are "over-trained" in the drill of life, and think "the

" game is not worth the candle." They want "that repose in mere
" sensation "* which life can never allow. There is a quiet hankering always stationed within them after Rest, an attachment to the
infinite hush they expect when clattering life goes out; their heart
is not in the play, and though for manners' sake they show a
pleasant face their feeling belies it. To think of the vast surroundings of machinery makes them sick: they see no End, and loathe
the means. Dead bodies look more at home than they ever did
" in life:" the drill of Art is over there, we see an air of amnesty to
all effort, and of standing at ease at last. Thus when men are tired
the thought of universal mechanism only tires them more; instinct
cries out against reminders of work, and tries to come to rest.

Again, to dissect a human body on a bright May morning, when
the sun comes in like amber, is a distasteful task to a tired mind.
It is so much more obvious to use our masterly powers of enjoying
Life than to audit the various accounts that compose the fund.
We are then retracing our steps from the present high standpoint,
inspecting the route along which we have worked our way. We
do not like the analysis, the barefaced exposure of machinery,
because we do not care to look back into the darkness of a very old
history of tiring struggle and weary work: we live in the current
chapter, and the whole course of the tale is too heavy a burden
for the consciousness of one generation. Out of doors enjoying
ourselves, or when reading wild rhetoric, we may pretend that
Consciousness comes and goes at its own sweet will, an unrelated
vagary; but when we have travelled through the regions of a
corpse we know better: the organism, though dead, speaks, and
tells its own tale. Then regarding the ruins, we see too bluntly
presented the blow of contrast, between the length of the ages
taken to learn the Art, and the shortness of the Life enjoyed: this
cuts and bruises our humour, and drives a ploughshare through
affection. Returning from the sight of death into the open air a
new present is made us, as we see Life going on fresh and bright,
unconscious of the underlying tragedy.

As a rule it is only young people who like machinery with a
zest; afterwards the contemplation seems to affect people with
a colder touch. Perhaps it is partly on this account that, as the
world grows older, it takes to *children* more and more; their
gestures breathe Hope, they are fresh to the play, and the air is
infected with freshness.

But besides this old-established aversion to machinery, there is
another, oftener seen in women than men. This is the objection to
" interference with Nature," with a view to making it better. It

---

* *Romola*, ch. 15, Bk. III.

arises from instinctive knowledge of how delicate a complication a living thing is, and a feeling that only godlike skill should lay its hand upon such art. But it is really appreciation of mechanism that is at the bottom of it, the consciousness, founded on experience, of the worth of a human (or other) organism, and the dread lest fools should rush in where angels fear to tread. This feeling, which every one must admire, opposed for some time the use of anæsthetics as an aid in childbirth, has put a veto on many sanitary suggestions, and has given force to the outcry against vivisection. We quote Shakespeare's description, when Perdita is explaining to Polixenes why she offers him "rosemary and rue," although it is hardly autumn and other flowers are out :—

Perdita.	"the fairest flowers o' the season
	Are our carnations, and streak'd gillyvors,
	Which some call nature's bastards : of that kind
	Our rustic garden's barren ; and I care not
	To get slips of them.
Polixenes.	Wherefore, gentle maiden,
	Do you neglect them ?
Per.	For I have heard it said,
	There is an art which, in their piedness, shares
	With great creating nature !
Pol.	Say there be ;
	Yet nature is made better by no mean
	But nature makes that mean : so, over that art
	Which, you say, adds to nature, is an art
	That nature makes. You see, sweet maid, we marry
	A gentler scion to the wildest stock ;
	And make conceive a bark of baser kind
	By bud of nobler race : this is an art
	Which does mend nature,—change it rather : but
	The art itself is nature.
Per.	So it is.
Pol.	Then make your garden rich in gillyvors,
	And do not call them bastards.
Per.	I'll not put
	The dibble in earth to set one slip of them :
	No more than, were I painted, I would wish
	This youth should say, 'twere well ;"

Agreeing as we do with "this youth" (*Florizel*) that everything Perdita did was right, we must accept both her opinions, the "*so it is*" with which she allows the argument as much as the charming indignation with which she returns constant to her first conviction. We admire her for the clean simplicity of health in what she says, and would rather she did not change her views. Her sentiment is a fine safeguard against the quackery of grafting cast-iron social schemes upon a world of flesh and blood : this unconscious caution of women's nature is what saves the world from the ludicrous effects that might otherwise often occur. They shrink from the "uncanny," from a brutal mechanical mixture instead of a real combination of nature; because they feel there can be nothing lasting in the result, no interlacing alliance of force, but an obliterating suicidal conflict. This sort of "art," that "shares with great creating nature" without the least real partnership, will endorse Perdita's scorn by the barrenness of its results.

But though Perdita spoke nicely as a girl, for men there is the other aspect of the question to be embraced. They have to put their shoulder to the wheel of the world's progress. Nature rises to higher things on stepping-stones afforded by herself: the share we take in this great "creating" process is to keep *trying*, till presently we find an opening through which nature is released; we set great natural tendencies—blind as they are powerful—at liberty. This is the art which *does*—when honest men are its disciples— mend nature, and change the face of the world for human beings : "but the art itself is nature." If our art however is unhappy enough to breed "bastard gillyvors" which are only monstrous abortions, they will suffer neglect by Time, and soon die out; and if when the complexion of humanity seems pale we can do nothing better than touch it superficially with a dead varnish like the "paint" that Perdita pictured on her face, the rubbing of cruel facts will soon take it off again. The real art is a different thing from artifice, and requires honest apprentices. There are no particular formulæ by which to ensure success in it; it seems to be vigorous in a soil where human warmth, straightforwardness, and patient sense abound. It does not object to higher latitudes.

Having now considered the two great reasons of a cold attitude towards Mechanism (we need not stop to answer that objection which has attached to the word "mechanical" associations of red tape, fixity, want of variety, and other stigmas : if men were only as susceptible to improvement, or progressed with as much variety, as the machines they make), the attitude itself begins to look very much like the "shying" of a horse. Coming round the corner of the nineteenth century, men were startled by an outburst of machinery ; but, taken gently up to face it, they sniff and find there is nothing uncanny after all.

Yet some people are heard to express a fear that before many years "the very air will be thick with machinery !" Is it not filled with it now ? outside us, as far as the east is from the west, and within us, in every blood corpuscle or nerve-cell, the whirr of mechanism never ceases. Does it trouble us? only when it goes wrong. We notice it about as much as the weight of that air which presses hard upon every inch of our bodies. What we *do* notice is the *consciousness* it brings : that bright silver which our bodies extract from the lead of Existence; that dazzling steel which flows from the organic "converter," and was once imprisoned with underground clay; that symmetrical pattern so prettily weaved from a yarn that was out-of-door fluff or discarded cocoon; that steady stream of glossy paper got from the very chaff of the universe. We enjoy the finished articles, but disdain recognition of the works; we are obsequious to the fortune, but too refined to remember how it was made.

Lastly, the man convinced against his will will not sit down till he has significantly asked, Is this the whole account of the matter? is this a real portrait of Life, or a pretentious caricature? We know what he means, and what he misses; yet we think the outline is there, the family characteristics, the general likeness. But to put the colour in, and run a rich reality of expression over the face, we can give no help beyond a few fragmentary hints.

> " 'Tis Love that makes the worlds go round.".

This is the first bit of insight, a saying as trustworthy as it is familiar. The second is a remark of Wordsworth, one of Nature's most intimate friends :—

> " We live by admiration."

The third is that much-abused assertion which we learnt to dislike in our copy-book days,

> " Where there's a will there's a way !"

With these three hints for clues we are led further towards the heart of things than with volumes of explanation. For though we shall not find "love" in the great stir of inorganic activities, yet there we shall see the same disposition of units and the same attitude of bodies towards each other which in ourselves we call by that name. A longing to get together, a universal greeting tendency, pervades every atom of the universe; from this come planets and caucuses, and the thousand kinds of commodities that load our ships.

And is not ordinary organic life (to say nothing of our own) kept up by those warm pulsations of Existence which, when they happen in ourselves, we call "admiration?" The bees so busy in the sun, the birds ecstatic in the April air, the horses rolling on the turf, the cattle in the shade enjoying their ruminant ease, the fragrant larch bursting out in buds of irrepressible growth, the hedges radiant with health beside the roads, the wild rose opening its lovely tints,—are not all these varieties of life sustained and fed by that response to the external world, that delight in their surroundings, which is admiration ? As for ourselves, we owe our existence to some previous admiration, and therefore literally do live by it : also the stronger that admiration was, the greater the power of life ; while again the more we admire the more we live.

The third quotation gives a glance down the avenues of Evolution. If love and admiration—or something simpler but akin to them—possess every bit of stuff in nature, we need not wonder at the fact that a way has been made from molecules up to men. For as love and admiration generate "will" in us, so their analogues occasion "energy" in the outside world; and there is then no lack of ways and means for moving towards the common end to which all individual things are by a common disposition impelled. But the end keeps retreating ; for as motion along the paths of energy brings greater reward, so a greater energy is born, and this impels to swifter flights again.

Thus love and mechanism seem to be inseparable, beginning together and advancing by means of each other. New love creates better mechanism : and better mechanism brings the power of greater love. Cymon was transformed by meeting Iphigenia : and while the seeds of plants are left to the mercy of bird or breeze, the human mother—not from greater kindness, but from greater ability—remains a mother till death. Love is the monarch of all ; and Mechanism his queen.

Finale.

There are spots on our English railways where the line is eloquent ; the stones and "sleepers" seem to speak.

If anyone would like to contrast certain triumphs of men over outside Nature with certain failures to manage inside nature, let him take a look some fine morning at those Westminster slums— not a stone's throw from the Houses of Parliament—where fate has rolled men into gutters, where rents kill modesty, and so dirt and disgrace are accepted good-humouredly as a matter of course— and then, turning his back on this, let him rattle up to St. Pancras in time for the 10.35 express, and by five in the afternoon step out in romantic Westmoreland.* When he has had some food, he should retrace his steps by rail up the ascent to Hawes Junction. Strolling out there on the shadowy hills as the sun begins to set, he has come to a gathering of pure Nature, and he stands alone with an assemblage of mute mountain-peaks. A little later, having walked to the top of the watershed, where rivulets rustle down the rocks, as he waits in the shelter where the Ure and Eden rise together, except for the faint crackling of the limestone crags he can almost hear the moonlight fall upon the stillness. Beside him is the railway, a strange intruder, and Bow Fell looks down calm on this triumph over difficulties. Then there issues an earnest uproar† from the milk-blue mist where Kirkby Stephen lies some miles lower down, and soon he sees three red lights diminishing past him till they vanish in the tunnel on the south.

At another part of the Midland route to Scotland, the land-scape is almost audible with expression. Between Carlisle and Hawick we have to climb 950 feet of the Lowlands, and get over forty-six miles, in an hour and five minutes. When we leave the curves of the Esk, and run into higher Liddesdale, as we steam with disciplined hurry up the sheltered slopes of this once inter-national valley, past the sheep feeding undisturbed in the sunshine that entertains the silence of the region, like boys who come home after a long absence to find the same old furniture and mantelpiece changed because they can now see over it, or get their chins above it, so we from our modern rapid seat regard the unaltered hills, while we charge along the open scarp of moor above Newcastleton up a gradient of 1 in 70 [for 8 miles in succession] with unbroken wind. And Mr. Smiles, speaking from the other end of the ancient boundary, where the Tweed and the North Sea foam beneath the Border Bridge, re-echoes this sentiment:—" The " warders at Berwick no longer look out from the castle walls " to descry the glitter of Southron spears. The bell-tower, from " which the alarm was sounded of old, though still standing, is " deserted; the only bell heard within the precincts of the old " castle being that of the railway porter announcing the arrival or " departure of trains. You see the Scotch express pass along the " bridge and speed southward on the wings of steam. But no " alarm spreads along the Border now. Northumbrian beeves are " safe. Chevy Chase and Otterburn are quiet sheep-pastures. " The only men-at-arms on the battlements of Alnwick Castle are " of stone. Bamborough Castle has become an asylum for ship-" wrecked mariners, and the Norman keep at Newcastle has been

† Appleby, arrive 5.20.
‡ 8 P.M. up express from Carlisle.

" converted into a Museum of Antiquities. The railway has
" indeed consummated the Union."*

If we stand on the High Level bridge at Newcastle, the wind
that blows up from the shipping below is charged with a melody for
which the rumble overhead makes a fitting accompaniment. The
tale of change is told here with dramatic power. The mountain-
stream beneath us is itself transformed; once a broad shallow
that a man could ford (not many years ago), it now affords depth
for the heaviest ships. Away up on the northern bank the Roman
Wall lies hid, dead as a forgotten habit, its arrowy route just marked
by a burial heave of the turf. Before us stands the massive Keep,
with sturdy Norman walls; the trains of the North-Eastern are
scrunching on the curve within a yard of it; Stephenson's engine
looks down on Elizabethan gables; behind us the steam-tram and
its noisy bell prepare to climb the Gateshead hill. From the mile-
long frontage of those world-known works that edge the water on
our west a steamer starts for Bilbao; as we follow her down the
seven miles of shipping to the sea, looking back on the land the
echoes of the past resound. We recall the early dates of our
railway calendar:—how the wooden-way was laid with iron, how
in the October of 1812 Hedley tried his tubs with men at the
handles inside Mr. Blackett's grounds, then made his first locomotive by February, 1813, and by May of the same year had a
successful one at work; how in 1814 Stephenson's first was—thanks
to Lord Ravensworth—constructed; how Mr. Dodds provided
funds for a second, turned out in 1815, which was a better copy
of its Wylam parent; how Mr. Losh helped him to patent improved
rails in 1816; how, after stubborn disappointments in planning the
Darlington line, in 1819 "a new survey was made, avoiding the
" Duke's fox-cover;" how Mr. Edward Pease and some other friends
of the world saw the Bill through Parliament in April, 1821; how
in 1823 power was obtained to use locomotives (for goods traffic),
and an amended line begun; how Stephenson and Pease started
their engine-factory at Newcastle in 1824; how the Stockton and
Darlington line was finally opened in September, 1825, the engine
drawing 38 wagons of passengers and goods; how, nevertheless,
after two years' experience, the Company were so dissatisfied that
they were on the point of reverting to horses; when in 1827,
Hackworth, a former workman of Hedley, made them the " Royal
" George," with Hedley's return-flue; how in 1828 the multitubular
boiler was patented in France by M. Sequin, and the same idea
suggested to Stephenson by Booth in 1829; how acting on these
ideas Stephenson won the Rainhill contest in October, 1829, and

---

* *Lives of the Engineers,* vol. iii, p. 415.

railways were now a certainty at last ;—and how all this was done
quietly in the country, 300 miles from London, unaided by Government—these incidents of sixty years ago sound clear above the
tumult of the times.   It is a comfort to remember that these things
were a common Gentile success, worked out not by men who
believed they were favourites of Providence, but by Englishmen,
who, breathing the air of a keen coast, and familiar from infancy
with the doing of difficult deeds, came to look upon the future with
a natural unquestioning vigour that brought it within their grasp.
It is this feature of the achievement that makes it a gold medal for
subsequent workers,—and imparts a warm touch to the easterly
wind as it blows across the chill North Sea.

Continuing south by the "East Coast Route," crossing deep
ravines where the trees hide the water, curving suddenly over the
bird's-eye view of beautiful Durham, and running along till we
lose the leisurely Wear, three-quarters-of-an-hour brings us to busy
Darlington, where even the Scotch express pays a tribute of three
minutes' stop. Here is the old focus of Stephenson's first labours,
and the pioneer line still faces the traveller to Stockton, the same
as sixty years ago, only now an unnoticed item in the crowd of its
descendants.   But the surrounding district has passed since then
through a wonderful transformation scene : Middlesbrough spreads
her streets of sixty thousand souls over ground that was then a
swampy waste, and the shifting estuary is now a compact harbour
The flames of towering furnaces watch through the night,—
pulsating on the stillness of romantic Saltburn miles away—while
from their fiery depths the native lias yields a ceaseless gift of iron
to the iron resolution that is native too.   The particular magic
which has come over the mouth of the Tees seems appropriate to
the spot where the railway spell was first put forth.

Fifty-four minutes through a tranquil plain, and we bend in
beside the Ouse to an exquisite picture.   There is half-an-hour to
wait at York, the whole of which need not be spent inside the
refreshment-room.   Outside, at the northern end of the platform,
is a sight as moving to an ordinary man as it is striking to an
artist.   Facing us are the old town, and older river, and the gray
Minster broods unvexed over the history of two thousand years.
The Yorkshire fields lying level around, the blue stream, flowing
tranquilly past the shadows of bridges and ancient irregular
houses, the massive tower, aloft with circling birds and sunshine,
the narrow old streets half hid by gables, the hillocks of red-tiled
roofs in various tints of age seen softening through the city
smoke, and the open plain beyond, stretching quiet in its own
fertility, except where here and there the sun-light shows an eager
train on one of the modern tracks that intersect its green expanse

—this picture has a special charm when we turn and contrast it with the busy stir of the platform. The weather-worn cathedral and the brand-new station are the two rival objects; but though outwardly unlike they are in sympathy with each other. Both show a belief in possibilities; the first, an early one, which, feeling only that there *was* a responsiveness somewhere outside, stretched upwards to the sky; while the second, a thousand years later, finds hope at its elbow, and so its work is diffused upon earth. An equally earnest energy may have planned the two, but the change of investment is caused by the arrival of definite knowledge. We look out again on the heirloom of St. Mary's Abbey and the older Roman arches, and the plaintive part of the suggestion dies away before the dozens of ruddy children who expatiate on the soft turf or run for hide-and-seek behind the ruins. Their healthy laugh rings out with the everlasting freshness of the race, as it comes back from its dip in Lethe,—while the blue water keeps on its patient way to the Humber.

But time is up, and we must leave this station, one of the tonic sights of England. The guard blows his whistle, the eight-foot wheel of the " G.N.R." revolves, the last smoker is shut in, and in a few seconds the " Scotchman " is straining away into distance as if nothing else were worth living for—just like a lover, with single-minded enthusiasm. Those who remember this express at York in the icy winter of 1879-80, when the few travellers who were not thawing themselves at the waiting-room fires used to stamp up and down a sawdusted platform under a darkened roof, while day after day the train came gliding in from Grantham with "couplings" like wool, icicles pendent from the carriage eaves, and an air of punctual unconcern, or those who have known some of our other equally sterling trains—these will hardly mind if friendship does let them drift into exaggeration when speaking of expresses. Who ever admired any living thing without describing it in terms a little extreme! From the weakness of such a "personal equation" no honest man need ever pray to be delivered. And to those who think this praise of expresses too arrogant and disproportionate, it may always be replied, What would England be without them ? It is difficult for anyone living now in the full sunshine of the *fait accompli* to have too much appreciation of that change concerning which calm Mr. Edward Pease, up before the dawn, made this pithy remark, " Let the country but make the " railroads, and the railroads will make the country."*

The country *did* make the "railroads," and we have tried to show how they are *making* the country,—a happy illustration of

* Smiles's *Lives of the Engineers*, vol. iii, chap. xvi.

that art which Perdita mistrusted. They are persuading into a
living whole with one heart and mind those insular insularities that
used to keep every part aloof from the rest. Individuals will have
more happiness because they will enjoy a national as well as an
individual life; and the nation will be something to be prouder of
when the entire life within it pulsates in one harmonious wave.
Concerted music gives more pleasure than discordant strains : we
have been listening now to the orchestra "tuning up;" and to some
people there is in this preliminary a special fascination (like the
charm that hovers round girls just new to their teens), for they see
the Future coming into focus through the present, they scent the
summer in the spring, they catch chaos shifting into creation, in
short they see a living thing in the very fact of *becoming*,—which
is the fact of facts, the quintessence of consciousness.

But we have overshot our platform, and must come back a
little. *Bradshaw* is the score of a symphony that goes on day and
night in the present. Let us look at this score.

Definition of "Express."

THE object of this paper is to give an account of the Express trains run in England. We must therefore first decide by what test we speak of a train as "express."

The words "*journey-speed*" will be used to denote the average number of miles per hour, *stoppages included*, by which a train advances on its journey : *e.g.*, the Great Northern "Scotchman" reaches Edinburgh nine hours after leaving King's Cross, a distance of $392\frac{1}{2}$ miles ; its *journey-speed* is therefore $43\frac{3}{8}$ miles per hour, or, shortly, "j.s. = $43\frac{3}{8}$."

Now on examining the various passenger trains in England, we shall find that though there are individual trains with "journey-"speeds" of every gradation from 15 to nearly 50 miles an hour, yet these arrange themselves naturally in three thickest clusters :—

	Miles per hour.		
Trains with a *journey-speed* of about........	15—25	{ "*Stopping*" trains .... }	Stop every, or nearly every station
	30—35	"*Fast*" ditto	Irregular in method, sometimes several stops, then a long run, &c.
	40 and upwards		Long spells of running; no lounging at stations

that is to say, trains with journey-speeds *between* 25 and 30, or between 35 and 40, are a thin percentage of those with journey speeds of 15 to 25, 30 to 35, or 40 and upwards.

Secondly, if we look at all those trains which the Companies themselves designate as "express," we see that seven-eighths of the aggregate have journey-speeds of "about 40 and upwards;" some small Companies it is true call trains "express" (the Brighton is a great offender) whose journey-speed—on ordinary gradients—is as low as 37, but the total number of such trains is relatively insignificant; others again (the Great Western, Great Eastern, and North Eastern) exhibit a few mongrel specimens which try to be both "stopping" and "express;" but the vigorous northern companies have sharp lines of demarcation.

Thirdly, the public mean "express" to mark distinction. But those who are familiar with English railways will admit that a train running over an average sample of our gradients and in ordinary circumstances, does not deserve distinction unless its journey-speed

R

is up to 40.* Now and then, where *gradients* are exceptional,—crossing the Pennine or over the Lowlands—we find a train with journey-speed as low as 37 or 36, and yet it must be called "express," because it keeps on and does all that can be done; in fact these runs are often the most admirable. Also, when *other circumstances* in the running of trains are not ordinary, as on the North Western where unusual stops occur at *Crewe* to make-up or break-up Liverpool and Manchester portions, or as on the Brighton and Great Eastern at *Croydon* and *Tottenham* respectively, where delays are inevitable for uniting or detaching the portions allotted to two London termini,—in cases like this, happily less than 10 per cent. of the whole, a train is still "express" though its journey-speed is only 39.

If then we draw the line of our definition where the trains themselves leave us most room, where the best Companies agree with us, and where it falls in with the general understanding, we see that an "*express*" is *a train whose "journey-speed," under ordinary conditions, comes up to 40 miles an hour.*

But, carrying out the spirit of this definition, which is simply to include all first-rate trains, as we have to allow for these cases when either gradients or other circumstances are extraordinary, our definition becomes 3-headed.

And so the trains collected and averaged in this paper will be either—

<table>
<tr><td rowspan="9" style="writing-mode:vertical">"Express" trains.</td></tr>
</table>

(a.) *The general rule;* those which run under ordinary conditions, and attain a journey-speed of 40 and upwards. These are about 85 per cent. of the whole.

(b.) Equally good trains, which, having to face *exceptional gradients*, only attain perhaps a journey-speed as low as 36 or 37. These are about 5 per cent. of the whole.

(c.) Trains which, not on account of gradients, but through unusually long *stoppages* or similar causes, only reach a journey-speed of 39. These are about 10 per cent.† of the whole.

No trains with a journey-speed less than 40 will be admitted unless the lower speed is caused by reasons (b) or (c). If it be asked why trains—running under ordinary conditions—with a journey-speed of not much below 40 are excluded, the answer is that there are so few of them in comparison, and that the definition is made accordingly; having made it, we must stick to it for the sake of order. All the trains *averaged* have a journey-speed as high as 40, except the small percentages which form classes (b) and (c). And the only trains absent from the following tables which yet are known as "exp." on their own lines or in public

* This only happens to be the standard just now; in ten years the majority of trains will probably have levelled up to a mile or two more.

† 10 per cent. of the *number,* but not of the *mileage,* of the whole; for most of this class run short journeys.

estimation, are one or two of the North Western *Manchester* trains, some of those to *Yarmouth* or *Norwich* on the Great Eastern, one or two on the Great Western and North Eastern, and five or six on the *Brighton* line.

" *Running-average* " (r.a.).

The term "running-average" must here be explained. By this is meant the *average speed* per hour while actually in motion *from platform to platform, i.e.,* the average speed obtained by deducting stoppages. Thus, the 9-hour (up) Great Northern "Scotchman" stops 49 minutes on its journey from Edinburgh to King's Cross, and occupies 8 hours 11 minutes in actual motion: its "running-average" is therefore 48 miles an hour, or, briefly, "r.a. = 48." The tabular statement for this train will thus appear:—

Distance in Miles.	Between	Time.	Journey-Speed.	Minutes Stopped.	Running-Average.
392½	Edinburgh and King's Cross	H. M. 9 0	43½	49	48

[*Digression.*—It must be noted that the "r.a." of a train will generally seem too low to those who have travelled by it. This is partly because in the "average" is included the slow speed at starting and stopping, or between ticket-platforms and the terminus, as well as any checks due to cautious running through suburbs (this affects the *Great Eastern* and *Brighton* lines in particular) and junctions, round sharp curves, over certain bridges and viaducts, &c. But the disappointment is chiefly owing to the fact that few people notice the *diminution of speed* in *running up gradients* (it requires practice to be much affected by the difference between 50 or 35 miles an hour), while the brilliant, though in consequence short, dashes down so impress the imagination (especially as we often finish with this, large towns being on low levels) that the journey seems to have been mainly composed of them. The average impression made on our consciousness is, in fact, much higher than would be made by the *uniform* continuance of a speed equal to the *average* of the different speeds at which we have been running;* thus the calculated "r.a." comes out a disappointment. This is strikingly shown in the case of the running between Carlisle and Hawick by the North British. Here, when we have once got up the long ascent of $\frac{1}{75}$ after Newcastleton, and, having passed the

---

* It is for this reason that the Great Western "Dutchman" deceives its passengers in a converse way. Between Paddington and Swindon, on a very smooth line free from gradients, the 55 miles from Taplow to Swindon are run within the hour, but as the speed is so uniform it attracts less attention, and most people are surprised if they consult their watches.

tunnel at the top, proceed to sweep down the descent at a pace that seems fabulous, the impression of speed remaining with us at the finish (repeated later when we drop on Edinburgh from the Fala Moors) is so intense that we are incredulous of the fact that the running-*average* has been only 42.

This is because we forget that in making an ascent away from the earth's centre, followed by a corresponding descent nearer it, we spend more minutes altogether than would have been required for running, with an equal expenditure of work, the same number of miles on a level. For suppose that an engine, which, working as hard as it can, makes 60 miles an hour on level, comes to an ascent. Suppose that while ascending, the earth annuls, and while descending the other side contributes, one-third of the speed on a level, *i.e.*, the engine goes up at one-third less, and comes down at one-third more, than 60 miles an hour. Going up at a speed one-third less, each mile must take *one and a half times* the number of minutes it would on level; while coming down at a speed one-third greater, each mile is done in *three-quarters* of the number of minutes it would take on a level. Half a minute is lost on each mile going up, and only one quarter of a minute saved on each going down: that is, compared with the same engine on level ground, one quarter of a minute extra is required for each two miles of the whole distance. Thus, spending more minutes than if the same distance were level, our *running-average* falls, for "running-"average" is the average space passed through each minute.

Or, again, it is obvious we go up hill slower than down, that a 10-mile ascent consumes *more minutes* than the 10-mile descent. And, therefore, *even assuming* that the extra speed added down hill is as great as that subtracted up, which cannot be in practice (see p. 105), still, as it produces its compensatory effect *during fewer minutes*, it cannot recover what was lost to an equal degree during each one of *more* minutes. During every minute of the ascent we are dropping behind our imaginary rival on the level; while during every minute of the descent we only gain on him in the same degree,—and there are fewer minutes in the descent. So the train on the level must, with an equal expenditure of work, beat us. Gradients exemplify the motto, "Heads I win, tails you lose;" but as the loss ends up so brilliantly (the station will be at the *bottom*), and the period during which the gradient was winning is several miles away, we are liable to miss the fact.

And thus there is nothing paradoxical in saying that, over English gradients on a fair sample of a line (not on an easy bit like the North Western from Liverpool to London), we need not be surprised to experience a few miles at 60 *miles an hour*, even though the "r.a." be no higher than 44 or 45. The "Dutchman" and the Scotch express over the North Eastern ought to maintain (as they do) a uniform high pace; but, as a rule, the log of our fast trains consists of long (measured by time) pulls up hill at 25—35 miles an hour, shorter spins of 50—55 on the level, and still shorter dashes down hill at 60 to 70 miles an hour; *and a " running-average " of 45 in England is generally a very smart performance.* Abroad such things never occur, except once or twice in the United States (chiefly on the Philadelphia and Reading line).

The " r.a." is the skeleton that gives us the outline of the speed; but this must be clothed in each case with the details of local knowledge concerning hills, junctions, stations, tunnels, &c., if we wish a real flesh-and-blood picture of what takes place in practice.]

Proceeding now with the definition given, *i.e.,* admitting no trains with a journey-speed less than 40 unless they can plead something exceptional *en route,* we shall examine each* Company in turn, and see—

1. The *number of distinct " express " trains* run by it, and the average of their—

 (*a.*) Times on journey. | (*c.*) Minutes stopped on way.
 (*b.*) Journey-speeds. | (*d.*) " Running-averages."

2. The resulting *express service†* between London‡ and the chief towns on the Company's route, *i.e.,* the number of journeys to and from London per day at express speed. Also the averages for these journeys.

3. The *Long Runs* made daily, *i.e.,* runs of at least 40 miles in length, and done at a running-average of at least 40. Their averages. Also the *longest* and *quickest* of these.

4. The express *mileage, i.e.,* the total number of miles run by trains whose journey-speed satisfies the definition of " express."

5. The log of its *best express.*

6. The *gradients* over which this running is done.

And we conclude with tables of the summary under each head,

---

* The *Lancashire* and *Yorkshire* is the only great Company with no " expresses." This is owing to the frequency and geographical situation of its towns, which hug the sides of the Pennine. In *Ireland* there are none.

† The express *service* of a given town may of course be much greater than that afforded by the trains run *on its own account.* Thus between *Rugby* and Euston there are 50 express journeys, contributed by expresses run on account of Scotland, Ireland, Liverpool, Manchester, and Birmingham. Rugby itself would hardly get one, so with *Peterborough, Derby,* &c.

‡ As a rule the number of *expresses* between any two towns is synonymous with the number of London expresses whose route lies through the towns. Except between Liverpool and Manchester, and between several places on the south-western fork of the Midland, there are in general no independent *local* express trains. But there are scores of " fast."

giving also the time of the quickest express between London and each of the most important towns in England.

Before beginning, a few words as to the reasons for which our expresses are run. The North of England, which created high speed, is still the chief occasion of fast trains. Lancashire and Yorkshire are responsible for the majority of our best expresses; and these are better than they might be because of London being at an extremity of the island. It is often an object with business men to go there and back, with time for action there, within the limits of a day. Hence, as the stirring towns in England are so far north, high speed becomes for them a necessary of life, and then a commonplace for all.

The distribution of our chief expresses (over the main routes) may be roughly stated :—

Between		Number of Distinct Expresses.	Com- panies.	Run by
Liverpool and Manchester there are		52	2	M.S. & L. and N.W.
,, and London	,,	48	4 {	N.W., Mid., G.N., G.W.R.
Yorkshire towns and London *	,,	26	3	G.N., Mid., G.E.
,, themselves....	,,	12	1	N.E.
Lanc. and Yorks. and Scotland	,,	7	2	Mid. and N.W.
,, S.W. of England †	,,	12	1	Mid.
Leeds and Derby, local............	,,	4	1	Mid.
L'pool and Buxton (business)	,,	2	1	Mid.
Scotland and London (through)	,,	23	3	G.N., Mid., N.W.
Birmingham and London............	,,	9	2	N.W. and G.W.
{ Cambridge itself and London	,,	7	1	G.N.
{ ,, Norwich and London‡	,,	11	1	G.E.
{ Colchester, &c., and London ‡	,,	6	1	G.E.
{ Ipswich, &c., and London‡	,,	8	1	G.E.
{ Sussex seasides and London (business men)	,,	16	1 {	L.B. & S.C. [S.E. runs one, St. Leonard's]
{ Kent seasides and London	,,	4	2	L.C.D. and S.E.
London and ports for Continent..	,,	18	3 {	L.C. & D., S.E., and G.E.
,, Exeter (for S.W.)..	,,	7	2	G.W. and L. & S.W.
,, Bristol itself............	,,	6	1	G.W.
Ireland and London	,,	4	1	N.W.
Glasgow and Edinburgh them- selves	,,	16	2	Cal. and N.B.
Crewe or Rugby and Euston §	,,	15	—	N.W.
		313	—	

* Not counting through *Scotch* trains.

† Liverpool and Derby, 4; Hull and Milford, 4; York and Bristol, 4.

‡ Most of these are on account of Norwich or Yarmouth, but are not *express* the whole distance.

§ These are meant for expresses to Liverpool, Manchester, or Birmingham, but are not fast enough *all the way* to be entered in these tables.

The companies that run "express" are 14 in number, and they arrange themselves thus :—

Four south of the Thames: South Western, Brighton, South Eastern, and Chatham and Dover.

The Great Western } both unlike other lines.
The Great Eastern }

The three great routes northwards: the Great Northern, Midland, and North Western.

The two English and three Scotch which help work the northern traffic: Manchester Sheffield and Lincolnshire, North Eastern; Caledonian, North British, and Glasgow & South Western.

We shall begin at the bottom of England and work upwards; and, speaking generally, as we go north we find better performances.

We take the census of all† the "express" trains running in England during the summer season of 1883, *i.e.*, those given in "*Bradshaw*" for August, 1883. In winter there is a falling off on some lines, chiefly those running to Scotland, or those serving fashionable seasides; but the fastest trains do not alter for the winter weather. There is altogether about 10 per cent. less express mileage run during winter than in summer. [No difference on the *Great Western* or the 4 *Southern* lines; 5 exp. less on the *Great Eastern*; 4 each less on the *Great Northern*, *Midland*, and *North Western*; no difference for the *M. S. & L.*; 4 less for the *North Eastern*; 2 less for each of the three *Scotch* lines. Total, 27 *trains* and 4,200 *miles* less, out of 409 trains and 42,000 miles.]

LONDON AND SOUTH WESTERN.

Distinct Expresses.

Miles.	Between.	Number.*	Average Time.	Journey-Speed.	Average Minutes Stopped.	Running-Average.
171½	Waterloo and Exeter	3 (1 up)	H. M. 4 10	41¼	18	44¼
		[Also 4 *Fast*	4 35	37½	27	41¼]

* *Up* and *down* reckoned separately; when the numbers each way are the same, the joint figure is simply stated; when more one way than the other, it is stated in a bracket.

† The 8.0 p.m. from King's Cross and 7.30 p.m. from Euston are not counted, as they are only "grouse" trains, which run about a month.

Note.—The working tables of the companies are the authority for correct *times* and *distances*. "Bradshaw" is wonderfully accurate for such a mass of details, but occasionally little errors (especially of distance) persist in type unnoticed.

These three Exeter expresses are the only ones run by the South Western. There is not one to either *Portsmouth*, *Southampton*, *Bournemouth*, or *Weymouth*. The quickest to those places are :—

Miles.			Time. H. M.	Journey-Speed.	
73½	Portsmouth, (Pop. 127,000)	(up)	1 55	38⅓	(8 average about 2·18 = 32¼ journey-speed)
79	Southampton ...	(down)	2 4*	38¼	(10 average about 2·21 = 33½ journey-speed)
115½	Bournemouth ..	(down)	3 9	36⅔	
145½	Weymouth ...	(down)	4 0	36⅓	

* In the year 1848 the quickest ran in 1 hour 50 minutes.

Express Service between London and Chief Towns (provided by Express and Fast Trains together).

Miles.	Between London and	Number.	Average			
			Time. H. M.	Journey-Speed.	Minutes Stopped.	Running-average.
171½	Exeter	3 (1 up)	4 10	41⅙	18	44⅓
83½	Salisbury	4 (1 up)	2 3	40¾	7	43
47¾	Basingstoke	13 (6 up)	1 8½	41⅘	2	43

Long runs (by express and fast) :—

There are 13, averaging 47⅛ miles, at 44⅜ running-average. The *longest* and *quickest* is from Yeovil Junction to Exeter (ticket platform), 48½ miles, in 63 minutes = 46⅕ running-average. (By three down trains)	3 Exeter and Yeovil 4 Waterloo and Basingstoke 6 Basingstoke and Vauxhall — 13 —

Express Mileage.—Reckoning the three expresses and the *Long runs* of the fast trains: 890 miles, with a running-average of 44.

Gradients.—The London and South Western Railway is almost level to *Basingstoke*, and gets steeper as it goes west, having 10 miles steeper than $\frac{1}{200}$ between Basingstoke and *Salisbury*, 19 miles between Salisbury and *Yeovil* (nine are $\frac{1}{100}$ or worse), and 35 miles between Yeovil and *Exeter* (eighteen of which are $\frac{1}{100}$ or worse). From Basingstoke to *Southampton* is one gentle ascent and descent. The "direct" route between *Woking* and *Portsmouth* is very steep (*Haslemere*, the summit, 460 feet), as out of 48 miles 26 are steeper than $\frac{1}{200}$, 10 of them (4 on end) being $\frac{1}{80}$.

Best Express.*

Miles.	Stations.		Time.		Speed between Stations.
			H.	M.	
—	Waterloo ....dep.		2	30	45½
47¾	Basingstoke ....arr.		3	33	
			3	36	46¼
66¼	Andover Junction ....dep.		4	0	
			4	2	43
83½	Salisbury		4	26	
			4	32	45
118	Sherborne......................................		5	18	
			5	19	
122¾	Yeovil Junction		5	26	
			5	28	46⅛
171¼	Exeter { Ticket platform		6	31	
			6	32	
171½	{ Queen-street		6	33	

Journey-speed = 42½.
Running-average = 45.

* The other *down* express is similar to this, but the *up* takes 4 hours 24 minutes, stopping 24 minutes. These Exeter expresses are continually undergoing slight alteration, but keep the same average. In 1879 the quickest time was 4 h. 4 min.

LONDON, BRIGHTON, AND SOUTH COAST.

This line has no chance of doing great things with such a short course, but it may be called a very smart line for speed, if we consider the large proportion of suburbs in most of the long runs.

The Brighton is remarkable for the exceptional number of very good trains it runs, which yet are not "express." As it is the *shortest* of our lines, the same items which so lower the "r.a." on any line must here make a larger proportional effect. But in these tables we are noting *results* rather than merit,—the mere fact of quick locomotion. Perhaps we may say in fairness that the 16 trains shown here as "Fast," would, if the Brighton had a longer course, step up and swell its list of "expresses." It would then show a list of 30 short expresses; but this would still be disfigured by the old-fashioned exclusion of *third-class* passengers from all its best trains.

The expresses on this line are often exceptionally heavy trains.

Distinct Expresses.

Miles	Between	Number.	Average: Time.		Journey-Speed.	Minutes Stopped.	Running-Average.
			H.	M.			
50½	Lond. Bridge and Brighton	4	1	10	43⅓	−¼	43¾
50¾	Victoria and Brighton	4	1	16	40	2	41
50	London Bridge and Lewes.	2 (down)	1	15	40	2	41
50¼	Victoria and Lewes	1 ,,	1	16	39⅔	–	39⅔
65½	London Bridge and Eastbourne	3 (2 up)	1	34	42	2	42½*
65¾	Victoria and Eastbourne....	1 (down)	1	36	41	2	42
		15	averaging		41⅓†	and	42†
	There are also these *Fast* Trains.						
—	London and Brighton	8 (2 up)	1	22	37	4	39
—	,, Lewes, &c. ...	7 (4 ,,)	1	22	36¾	3	38
60	,, Worthing	1 up	1	35	38	5	40
		16	averaging		37	and	38¾
	Express Service between London and Chief Towns.						
50⅝	Brighton	8	1	13	41¼	1	42
50⅛	Lewes....................................	6 (down)	1	14	40½	1	41
65½	Eastbourne	4 (2 up)	1	34½	41⅓	1½	42½

* One of these, the 9.55 up, if we consider weight of train, sharp curves at *Polegate*, *Keymer*, and *Lewes*, the junctions and suburbs passed in such a short journey, is the smartest express in the S. of England.

† In taking these averages for the journey-speed, *each journey* counts as a *unit*, whether long or short, but for the running-average *every mile* counts at its own speed.

Long Runs.—There are 25, averaging 46 miles, at 42 r.a., (44 outside Croydon). *Longest*, from Eastbourne to London Bridge, 65½ miles in 1 hour 27 minutes = 45 r.a. (9.55 up). *Quickest*, London Bridge to Brighton, 50½ miles in 1 hour 5 minutes = 46⅗ r.a. (48 outside Croydon: 5 p.m. down).

Express Mileage.

15 express trains, running..	815	miles at	42	r.a. (44 outside London)
11 other Long Runs, making	455	,,	41½	,,
Total.	1,270	,,	41¾	,,

Gradients.—Of the four southern lines the Brighton has the easiest track. The only steep bit is from *New Cross* to *Forest Hill*—2½ miles of $\frac{1}{100}$. There are three other ascents and descents, on each side of the *Merstham*, *Balcombe*, and *Clayton* tunnels, all of $\frac{1}{164}$, each rise and each fall measuring respectively about 8, 5, and $4\frac{1}{2}$ miles. The remaining 13 miles are nearly level.

Best Express.

London Bridge   5   0 } $46\frac{3}{4}$ running-average (this is about 48 running-
$50\frac{1}{4}$ Brighton   6   5 }   average *beyond Croydon*).

SOUTH EASTERN.

The S. Eastern trains start from *Charing Cross*, but on account of the delays caused by crossing and re-crossing the Thames to Cannon Street, the express journeys are reckoned as beginning and ending at this latter station.

The S. Eastern and the Chatham & Dover run 7 expresses each between London and *Dover*, and 2 each between London and *Ramsgate*, &c. The S. Eastern also runs 2 more Continental trains between London and *Folkestone*, and the Chatham & Dover 2 between London and *Queenboro'*, but these latter are not "express."

Distinct Expresses.

Miles.	Between	Number.	Average			
			Time.	Journey-Speed.	Minutes Stopped.	Running-Average.
$74\frac{1}{2}$	Cannon St. & Dover (Town)	7 (4 up)	H. M. 1 45	$42\frac{1}{2}$	$\frac{1}{2}$	$42\frac{1}{2}$
69	,, Folkestone ,,	2 (tidal)	1 45	$39\frac{1}{2}$	–	$39\frac{1}{4}$
$83\frac{3}{4}$	London Bridge & Ramsgate	2	2 9	39	6	$40\frac{3}{5}$
59	St. Leonards & Lond. Bridge	1 (up)	1 32	$38\frac{1}{2}$*	2	$39\frac{3}{5}$
	Total	12	averaging	$41\frac{1}{8}$	and	$41\frac{3}{4}$

* Admitted because of gradients. See below.

Express Service to chief towns is represented above.

Long Runs.—There are 12, averaging $66\frac{1}{4}$ miles, at $42\frac{2}{3}$ running-average. The *longest* and *quickest* is between Cannon Street and Dover, $74\frac{1}{2}$ miles, in 1 hour 39 minutes = 45 running-average.

4 Dover and Cannon Street	1 Staplehurst and Cannon Street	
2 Shorncliffe and Cannon Street	2 Folkestone ,,	
2 Canterbury and New Cross	—	
1 Ashford and London Bridge	12	

Express Mileage.

12 expresses, running   885   miles at $41\frac{1}{4}$ running-average
1 Long run besides   54   ,, $41\frac{1}{2}$ (Ashford to London Bridge)

Total   940   ,, $41\frac{3}{4}$ running-average

Gradients.—The South Eastern has steep gradients, except between *Tunbridge Junction* and *Ashford,* where the line runs nearly at sea level and quite straight for 20 miles. From *New Cross* to the *Halstead* summit there is a 12-mile pull, mostly $\frac{1}{130}$ or $\frac{1}{140}$, and a 6-mile drop averaging $\frac{1}{130}$ from *Sevenoaks* tunnel to *Tunbridge Junction.* Beyond *Ashford* is a long easy descent of 11 miles, past *Shorncliffe* and *Folkestone,* to *Dover.* On the branch from Tunbridge Junction to *Hastings* there are continual severe ascents and descents, half the distance being $\frac{1}{132}$ or steeper ($\frac{1}{88}$ short bit); of the entire run from London to Hastings one-half averages about $\frac{1}{130}$.

Best Express.

Miles.			Time.	Speed between Stations.
			H. M.	
—	Cannon Street... dep.		7 48*	
74$\frac{1}{4}$	Dover .... arr.		9 27	45

* When the times given differ from those in "*Bradshaw,*" they are taken from the official working tables of the various companies.

LONDON, CHATHAM, AND DOVER.

Distinct Expresses.

Miles.	Between	Number.	Average			
			Time.	Journey-Speed.	Minutes Stopped	Running-Average.
			H. M.			
78	Victoria and Dover	7 (4 up)	1 52	41$\frac{3}{4}$	3	43
72	,, Westgate-on-Sea	2	1 41	42$\frac{3}{4}$	2	43$\frac{3}{4}$
	Total	9	averaging	42	and	43$\frac{1}{4}$
	Express Service between London and Chief Towns.					
79	Ramsgate	2	2 —	39$\frac{1}{2}$	8	42$\frac{1}{4}$
78	Dover...................................	7 (4 up)	1 52	41$\frac{3}{4}$	3	43
73$\frac{3}{4}$	Margate................................	2	1 45	42	4	43$\frac{3}{4}$
61$\frac{3}{4}$	Canterbury	4	1 28	42	2$\frac{1}{4}$	43$\frac{1}{4}$
34	Chatham	8 (1 up)	— 51	40	2	41$\frac{3}{4}$

Long Runs.—There are 8, averaging 63 miles, at 45 running-average. The *Longest* is Dover to Victoria, 78 miles, in 1 hour 45 minutes = $44\frac{3}{5}$ running-average. *Quickest* is Herne Hill to Dover, 74 miles, in 1 hour 36 minutes = $46\frac{1}{4}$ running-average.

1 Dover to Victoria	3 Herne Hill to Canterbury
1 Herne Hill to Dover	1 Dover to Chatham
2 " Westgate	8

Express Mileage.—Nine expresses, running 690 miles at $43\frac{1}{8}$ running-average ($44\frac{1}{2}$ outside Herne Hill).

Gradients.—The Chatham and Dover is the steepest average of any of the main lines of the four Southern companies. Of the 78 miles from Victoria to Dover, nearly 50 are between $\frac{1}{100}$ and $\frac{1}{132}$, and only 18 easier than $\frac{1}{200}$. The line begins with a 27-mile ascent, broken by four minor descents, to *Sole Street* (300 feet), then dips up and down in short breaks to *Canterbury*, from which it rises 9 miles to *Shepherd's Well* (290 feet) and drops 7 miles into *Dover*. The gradients, though so incessant and steep, are not sufficiently long at a time to lower the speed much. The running-average of the best trains is however very creditable.

Best Express.

Miles.		Time. H.	Time. M.	Speed between
—	Victoria .... dep.	7	40	
4	Herne Hill .... arr.	7	47	
	dep.	7	49	} $46\frac{1}{4}$
78	Dover (Town)	9	25	

Journey-speed = $44\frac{3}{5}$ Running-average = $45\frac{1}{8}$

Summary of the Four Southern Companies.

	Expresses.	Long Runs.		Miles.	Total Express Mileage.	Running-Average.	
Lond. and South Western...	3	13	averaging	$47\frac{1}{3}$	890	at	44
Brighton	15	25	"	46	1,270	"	$41\frac{3}{4}$
South Eastern	12	12	"	$66\frac{1}{4}$	940	"	$41\frac{3}{4}$
Chatham and Dover	9	8	"	63	690	"	$43\frac{1}{8}$
Total	39	58	"	$52\frac{4}{5}$	3,790	"	$42\frac{1}{2}$

These four lines are, from an English point of view, very sparing of express trains, yet the above total shows an amount of speed of high quality equal to the joint contributions of the entire continent of Europe.

In proportion to the respective lengths of their systems, the results given above are best for the Chatham and Dover, worst for the *South Western.* This latter line is strangely destitute of expresses, as Southampton has found to its cost. Portsmouth, besides being a place of unique importance, is the only town in England with a population of 100,000 and not one train at 40 miles an hour.

The *Brighton* is the most brisk of the four Companies, but the presence of enormous fares in its express programme and the absence of third class (often second) passengers from it, cut away all ground for praise. The four trains that are lighted by electricity are " limited " to first class passengers, who pay 3*d.* a mile *plus* the Pullman charge, and yet in return for so much money there is little speed, as the running-average of the four is only 40½! The one great merit of this Company is its enterprise in the matter of sound continuous brakes. It was the first in England to introduce an effective one, and all its trains are now fitted with the Westinghouse.

The best point about the *South Eastern* is its service to Paris, *viâ* Folkestone. This journey of 258 miles is at present done in 8 hours 20 minutes, a journey-speed of 31 miles an hour, land and sea and all delays included. The fine steel steamers used go faster than many of the Company's trains on land. The great blots on the South Eastern are its unpunctuality, its fares, its third class carriages, and the way in which *local* interests are sacrificed to continental traffic. Behind the nine continental expresses stands out a background of the dreariest, slowest trains in England. This is a specimen of a line eager to " tap " traffic, but not to encourage it.

The little *Chatham and Dover* is to be praised for the spirited way in which it runs over its hilly route. But during a great part of the year it is wasting its substance on the seven Dover expresses, while duplicates of these are running at identical times on the neighbouring South Eastern. These 14 Dover expresses merely divide, and do not breed, any continental traffic; for none of them are third class, and the fares are excessive.

Speaking generally, the four Southern lines do not take kindly* to expresses, but seem to run them under protest, as compared with the spontaneous speed of the North of England. Then there

---

* For even the Brighton, though it shows an express disposition, persists in the old idea of making people pay extra for the exceptional mercies of high speed.

is a worse feature peculiar to these four companies, that is, their enormous fares. The utility of an express depends not more on its speed than on the low price at which we can avail ourselves of it. But, with the exception of the three L. & S.W. Exeter and the four Ramsgate trains, all the expresses of the Southern lines close their doors to third class passengers. Thus their service to the public becomes attenuated to a shadow of what it might be. Not content with this exclusion, they proceed to charge those whom they do carry fares which are phenomenal. We subjoin a few instances of the price charged for carrying people similar distances *by express* in the case of Northern and Southern companies respectively :—

Miles.	Between	Fares (single).			Daily Service. Counting Up and Down separately.
		1st Class	2nd Class.	3rd Class.	
					With an avge. r.a. of
50½	London and Brighton (L.B.& S.C.) .	12/3	8/6	(none)	8 expresses 42
49¾	,, Bedford (Midland)........	6/7	—	3/11½	17 ,, 45½
47¼	Edinburgh and Glasgow (N.B.) ...	6/6	5/-	2/6	
78	Victoria and Dover (L.C. & D.)	20/-	15/-	(none)	7 ,, 43
75½	Charing Cross and Dover (S.E.R.)....	20/-	15/-	(none)	7 ,, 42¾
76¾	King's Cross and Peterboro' (G.N.R.)	11/3	8/9	6/4	29 ,, 48⅛
83½ 82¾ & 84¾	Waterloo and Salisbury (L.S.W.) .... Euston and Rugby (L.N.W.)...........	17/6 12/9	12/3 9/10	6/11½ 7/2	4 ,, 43 50 ,, 44⅔
73½ 73½	Waterloo and Portsmouth (L.S.W.) Carlisle and Carstairs (Cal.)	15/- 12/4	10/6 9/3	(none) 6/1½	No express at all 9 expresses 43

Note.—In this last case, the gradients on both lines are very steep, but on the Portsmouth line they are short, the highest point being about 450 feet, while the Caledonian has a sharp pull up to over 1,000 feet, the last ten miles averaging $\frac{1}{80}$. Yet the Caledonian does its journey in 18 *minutes less* of actual running time.

Thus we see that south of the Thames people pay from half as much again to nearly double what they pay north of it, though the speed in the latter case is so much superior. In railway matters all items of excellence flourish or pine together. The comparatively sorry picture of fewer expresses, higher fares, more unpunctuality, and inferior carriages, to be observed south of the Thames, is a reflection on the people for whom the trains are run.* The North of England towns would not submit to these services, but the

* It is only fair to add that the Brighton line is much the least unpunctual of the four Southern ones; this bears out the general fact that those lines which run the most expresses are the most punctual,—simply because they must be—for the Brighton runs most of the four.

crowds of individuals who breathe London air seem incapable of that joint energy which in other localities would soon put an end to such grievances.

We now come to the

GREAT WESTERN.

This is a line of its own sort. It runs both north and south of the Thames, exhibits a corresponding mixture of characteristics, and is altogether anomalous. Its best trains are among the very first in England, but it is, in proportion to its size (much the biggest in the kingdom), more destitute of expresses than any line except the South Western. It offers instances to show what it *could* do, and then proceeds not to do it. But it is improving a little at present, and may soon show a sight more worthy of its permanent way, which is one of the most favourable for express running.

The present "express" service of the G.W.R. consists of the 2 excellent *Birkenhead* trains, the 4 *Exeter*, (the 2 afternoon ones are called "Zulu," because they began to run the day after the Prince Imperial was killed—the 2 morning ones are the "Dutchman"), 6 others between *Bristol* and Paddington, 2 others between *Birmingham* and Paddington, and 1 *Irish* boat-express, which, however, is not fast beyond Cardiff. There are also 2 quick *Weymouth* trains, express only between Paddington and Swindon. *Swansea, Cardiff,* and *Birmingham,* with their population of half a million, might have been expected to command more than a total of *five* expresses from a great Company.

Distinct Expresses.

Miles.	Between	Number.	Average			
			Time.	Journey-Speed.	Minutes Stopped.	Running-Average.
			H.　M.			
246½	Paddington and Plymouth	4	6　7	40¼	40	45¼*
228	,,　　　Birkenhead..	2	5　16	43⅓	19	46
170½	,,　　　Cardiff (5.45)	1 (down)	4　21	39¼	25	43¼
129¼	,,　　　Birmingham	2	3　6½	41½	9½	43¾
118½	,,　　　Bristol	6	2　57½	40	18	44½
77	Swindon and Padd.(Wey.exp.)	2	1　52½	41	6	43⅓
75½	Exeter & Bristol (4.55 N. mail)	1 (up)	1　50	41¼	6	43¼
	Total	18	averaging	40¾	and	44¼
	Or, reckoning the Plymouth expresses only between *Exeter* and Paddington .... }	—	,,	42	,,	46¼

* This is the running-average *throughout*, but in justice to the trains it should not be reckoned beyond Exeter, where gradients are so heavy ($\frac{1}{47}$) and curves so sharp that express running is out of the question. The running-average of the four Plymouth trains *between Exeter and Paddington* is as high as 50¼.

Express Service to Chief Towns.

Miles.	Between London and	Number.	Average			
			Time.	Journey-Speed.	Minutes Stopped.	Running-Average.
			H. M.			
246¼	Plymouth	4	6 7	40¼	40	45¼
228	Birkenhead	2	5 16	43½	19	46
220	Torquay	4	5 21	41	40	47
213	Chester	2	4 57½	43	16¼	46¼
194	Exeter	4	4 15	45¾	23	50¼
171	Shrewsbury	2	3 53½	44	12½	46¼
170¼	Cardiff ⎱	1	4 21	39¼	25	43¾ *
158¼	Newport ⎰	1	21 min. less	—	—	
129¼	Birmingham	4	2 56	44	7	46
120	Worcester	1 (down)	2 58	40½	18	45 †
118¼	Bristol	10	2 49	42	16	46½
114	Gloucester.................	1 (down)	2 53	39½	14	43 ‡
106¾	Bath	10	2 30	42¾	13	46¾
77	Swindon................. ...	13 (6 up)	1 40¾	46	3¼	47¾
63	Oxford	5 (2 „)	1 28	43½	2	44¼
122½	Cheltenham	watering place { quickest 3.15 = 37¾ journey-speed				
168	Weymouth	„ { quickest 4.20 = 38¾ journey-speed				have no "express" service
216	Swansea................... {	with population of 65,000, quickest 6.0 = 36 journey-speed				
285¼	Milford .... {	on the straight route to Ireland from the south of England, quickest 8.0 = 35¼ journey-speed				

* Milford boat train. † 4.45 from Paddington to Birkenhead.
‡ Milford train.

Long Runs. There are twenty-four, averaging 56 miles, at a running-average of 48½ :—

6 Paddington and Swindon	1 Oxford and Birmingham
6 Bristol and Taunton	2 Shrewsbury and Chester
2 Swindon and Reading	1 Leamington and Oxford
2 Didcot and Paddington	1 Gloucester and Newport
3 Oxford and Paddington	24

Longest and quickest.—Swindon to Paddington, 77⅛ miles, in 1 hour 27 minutes = 53⅛ running-average (done four times).

Express Mileage.—Eighteen expresses, running 2,600 miles, at 46¼ *running-average* (reckoning none *beyond* Exeter).

Gradients. The Great Western has very easy gradients as a rule. Between *Paddington* and *Exeter* seven-eighths of the distance is practically level (a short drop between *Wotton Basset* and *Dauntsey*, another through *Box Tunnel*, each 2 miles of $\frac{1}{100}$, with an easier rise and fall between Bristol and Nailsea, and again

F

between Wellington and Tiverton Junction, are the chief gradients). From *Exeter* to *Plymouth* both curves and gradients are very severe—several miles of $\frac{1}{40}$—while between *Plymouth* and *Penzance*, curves, gradients, and wooden viaducts make such a combination, that the quickest train can only get snatches of speed against a background of caution.

The main line from *Didcot* to *Birkenhead* is also very level as a whole; short spells (1 or 2 miles at a time) of $\frac{1}{100}$ occur frequently north of Birmingham, and 4 miles of $\frac{1}{82}$ between *Wrexham* and *Rossett*.

On the third main line, between *Swindon* and *Milford*, there is a steep ascent on each side of the tunnel near *Stroud*, and frequent short bits varying from $\frac{1}{80}$ to $\frac{1}{100}$ west of Cardiff, but nothing sufficient to excuse the absence of expresses.

The Great Western Railway is unique in its track, which is broad gauge (7 feet) from Paddington to Penzance—mixed gauge as far as Exeter—and most of its system is laid with the *longitudinal* sleepers.

Best Express.

Miles.	Broad Gauge "Zulu."	Time. H. M.	Speed between	Miles.	Narrow Gauge.	Time. H. M.	Speed between
—	Paddington, dep.	3 –	53⅕	—	Paddington ....dep.	4 45	48⅘
77	Swindon	4 27		63½	Oxford	6 3	
		4 37	47			6 7	49⅓
106¾	Bath..................	5 15		129¼	Birmingham	7 27	
		5 20	44			7 30	38⅔
118½	Bristol	5 36		141½	Wolverhampton ...	7 49	
		5 41	52⅗			7 52	44⅝
163¼	Taunton	6 32		171¼	Shrewsbury...........	8 32	
		6 35	47⅓			8 35	46
194	Exeter	7 14		213½	Chester	9 30	
		7 18				9 33	44¼
246½	Plymouth....arr.	9 –	—	228¼	Birkenhead	9 53	
				—	Liverpool (ferry)	10 10	—
Journey-speed = 45¾, Running-average = 50⅓ (three others like this)				Journey-speed = 44½, Running-average = 47 (one other Up a little slower than this). This is in all respects the finest train by the Great Western			

The Great Western has not yet entirely emerged from its state of transition. A short time ago it was an unprofitable tangle of separate lines, for the most part ill-conditioned and with miserable accommodation. Now it forms a compact organism of 2,300 miles, with first-rate carriages and permanent way. When the Severn Tunnel is finished, and also that under the Mersey, we may look for two more batches of express trains. It has the smoothest running track in the kingdom, and the speed between Paddington and Swindon is the highest of any long run in England.* For years the Great Western was far ahead in the van of speed, these "Dutchman" trains running just as they do now about twenty years ago. This was the more wonderful as the permanent way and rolling stock on some parts of the route were decidedly below par.

The reason why the Great Western, which is so scantily supplied with expresses, has those few so very good, is to be found in the fact that its route to many important towns is much longer† than that of the competing lines. Thus the Birkenhead train runs to *Birmingham* in only 7 minutes more than the quickest North Western express, though the route from Paddington is 16 miles longer, and to *Shrewsbury* in 1 minute less, the distance being 8 miles more; to *Exeter*, with a route 22½ miles longer than the South Western, and stopping 5 minutes more on the way, it takes only 11 minutes more.

Owing to the wide intervals between expresses on the Great Western, the general keynote of the service is pitched very low. Porters handle luggage with heartfelt inertia, and the "Dutchman" is kept waiting *en route* in a way unknown in northern latitudes. This train can run well and easily within its time, but whether early or late there is a slackness in its treatment which contrasts strongly with the smart discipline of the other great lines.

"Express fares" were abolished on the Great Western about a year ago, and all its trains are now third class, except the four Exeter expresses and the two limited mails.

Weight of trains, and *Punctuality*.—So far we have hardly considered the *weight* of expresses, chiefly because, in the case of 3 at least of the 4 Southern lines, *unpunctuality* is the feature which swamps all other considerations. But, with companies who more or less carry out what they promise on paper, the speeds must be partly determined by the load to be drawn. We shall now therefore remind the reader of the necessity of noticing the average loads pulled by the great companies north of the Thames. The *Great Western* expresses are, as a rule, much the lightest of those

* But in the summer of 1880 the Great Northern ran four Leeds expresses, which did the distances between Grantham and Wakefield, 70 miles, in 1 hour 18 minutes, or 53¾ miles an hour, which is slightly faster than the Swindon runs.
† "G.W.R." is proverbially rendered "Great Way Round."

of any large company. Their punctuality is good, though easily overthrown.

GREAT EASTERN.

This again is a line which has lately undergone a pleasant metamorphosis from a state of ludicrous inefficiency into that of a well-equipped and promising express line. It has established a thoroughly good permanent way, built some masterly engines, fitted every train with the Westinghouse brake, and initiated a fresh service to Doncaster. Owing to the crowded suburban traffic which throngs its approaches to London,* the first 6 miles have to be run over at such a cautious speed that the "r.a." of expresses is considerably reduced thereby. Unless we bear this in mind, as well as the sharp curves on the Cambridge line, and the slackenings for junctions, bridges, &c., on the Colchester one, the running averages will not give a fair idea of the actual speed over most of the journey.

There are four groups of G.E.R. expresses :—

a. Six for *Doncaster* (worked by G.E.R. over the joint line, *viâ* Sleaford).

b. Those on the Ipswich line, for *Norwich* or *Yarmouth.* [None of these is " exp." *throughout*, and they therefore appear in the subjoined table as expresses for *Colchester* and *Ipswich* respectively.]

c. Those on the Cambridge line. [Only one is " exp." through to *Norwich*, and the remainder are given below as if they were all expresses on behalf of *Cambridge* itself.]

d. The 2 *Harwich* Boat Trains. [These are not strictly "exp.," but are admitted on account of the extenuating conditions which are so numerous on the Great Eastern. p. 80.]

These trains (except the *Doncaster* ones) are unusually long, but nevertheless run at very high speeds when clear of impediments. No better plan can be given to show a man how fine a thing a ' running-average " of 44 or 45 really is in England than for him to travel by any of the Doncaster trains. At first after the journey he will believe the "r.a." is wrongly calculated, and then he will begin to appreciate properly those grander speeds on the *Great Northern* or *Midland* represented by an "r.a." of 48—50

---

* The Chairman recently said that if they could only accommodate " 1,000 " trains per day " in and out of Liverpool Street, they would all be filled.

(pp. 85, 89, 107, 108, &c.). The Doncaster expresses of the G.E.R. are also interesting for this reason, that their joint "r.a." (44⅓) is exactly the same as the *average* "r.a." of the *whole* of the English expresses (see Table I, p. 110). They may thus be offered as a fair average sample of our present attainments in the way of speed.

The Great Eastern, when unharassed by floods, is a most *punctual* line.

Distinct Expresses.

Miles.	Between	Number.	Average: Time.		Journey-Speed.	Minutes' Stopped.	Running-Average.
			H.	M.			
*180¼—181	Liverpool Street and Doncaster	6	4	24	41	20	44⅓
†55½—56¼	London and Cambridge	10(4 up)	1	21½	41¼	2½	42½‡
124	St. Pancras and Norwich (Thorpe)	1 (d.)	3	10	39⅛	14	42¼
163	Norwich (Trowse) and Doncaster........	2	3	42½	44	14½	47 §
68¾	Liverpool St. and Ipswich	8	1	43	40	3¾	41½‖
51¾	" Colchester	5(2 up)	1	14	42	½	42¼‖
69¼	" Harwich (Continental)	2	1	48	38½	—	38½¶
		34	averaging		41	and	43¼

* According as they stop at *Sleaford* or run through by the loop.
† Liverpool Street and St. Pancras.
‡ Two others up, 1 hour 27 minutes = 38¼ journey-speed (not "exp.").
§ "Fast seaside train" (in summer only).
‖ Some of these *should* be Yarmouth and Norwich expresses.
¶ The last few miles run slowly.

Express Service to Chief Towns.

Miles.	Between London and	Number.	Average: Time.		Journey-Speed.	Minutes Stopped.	Running-Average.
			H.	M.			
180½	Doncaster	6	4	24	41	20	44⅓
143½	Lincoln	6	3	31½	40¾	15	43⅞
124	Norwich, *viâ* Ely...	1 (down)	3	10	39⅛	14	42¼
114	" *viâ* Ipswich	*none;* 4 av.	3	4 =	37⅛	—	—
121½	Yarmouth................	*none;* 1 up	3	21 =	36¼	—	—
68¾	Ipswich	8	1	43	40	3¾	41½
55½—56¼	Cambridge	17 (7 up)	1	20½	41¾	2	42⅘
51¾	Colchester...............	13 (5 up)	1	13½	42¼	−½	42½

Long Runs.—There are twenty-four, averaging 56¾ miles, at 42½ running average (44½ outside suburbs) :—

7	Liverpool Street and Colchester		2	Kentish Town and Cambridge
1	„	Mark's Tey	1	St. Pancras and Cambridge
2	„	Ipswich	2	Ely and Trowse
2	„	Harwich	1	Norwich and March
6	„	Cambridge	24	

The *Longest* is from Liverpool Street to Parkeston Quay, 69¼ miles, in 1 hour 46 minutes = 39½ running-average; from Liverpool Street to Ipswich, 68¾ miles, in 1 hour 40 minutes = 41¼ running-average; and from Trowse to March, 68½ miles, in 1 hour 27 minutes = 47¼ running-average (seaside train). The *Quickest* is between Lincoln and Spalding, 38¼ miles, in 47 minutes = 48¾ running-average.

Express Mileage.—Thirty-four expresses run 3,040 miles, at 43¼ running-average (45 outside suburbs).

[*A propos* of the Great Eastern, we must note that the "running-"average" of the tables in this paper gives merely what the speed amounts to from *platform to platform;* but in order to compare the "r.a." of different lines with a view to their proper relative appreciation, we must in each case look at the "r.a." through the medium of those various personal peculiarities of the line which prevent uniform speed, *e.g.,* gradients, crowded suburbs, junctions to slacken past, sharp curves, swing bridges, &c. (See also p. 61.)]

Gradients.—From Liverpool Street to Norwich, *viâ* Ely, is very easy running. The line rises imperceptibly for 30 miles to *Bishop's Stortford;* rises 5 more steeply (the last 2 averaging $\frac{1}{150}$) to *Elsenham,* 230 feet above sea; falls 4 miles, averaging $\frac{1}{250}$, to *Newport;* rises slightly to the *Audley End* tunnels, and falls 15 miles (first 3 averaging $\frac{1}{150}$) gently past *Cambridge* to the 58th mile. From this there is, except for crossing streams, &c., a dead level of 30 miles to the 88th mile (2 miles past *Brandon*), then a series of four easy ups and downs, and a sharper drop past *Hethersett* (3 miles averaging $\frac{1}{150}$); level the last 4 miles into Norwich.

The route from Ely to Doncaster is mostly nearly level. From Ely to *Sleaford,* 53 miles, it is in the Fens; between Sleaford and *Lincoln* it rises a little on to the oolite; and from Lincoln to *Doncaster* again is not far from sea level.

The Colchester route begins with a 19-mile gentle rise (but the last 3 average $\frac{1}{150}$) to *Brentwood,* 240 feet, and a gentle fall of 11 miles to *Chelmsford;* the next 22 miles, to *Colchester,* are level or easy undulations; then steeper ups and downs (averaging $\frac{1}{150}$

to $\frac{1}{110}$) of 3 or 4 miles in length for the next 28 miles; after which, for 30 miles, from *Melton* to *Beccles*, the line is broken up into little ripples, half a mile or a mile long, of steep gradients, averaging worse than $\frac{1}{100}$; and from Beccles, 12 more, less steep, into *Yarmouth*.

(This line follows the curve of the east coast, and is thus continually crossing (little) transverse valleys; the greatest height between Colchester and Yarmouth is only about 125 feet above sea, near *Westerfield*.)

Best Express.

Miles.		Time.		Speed between
		H.	M.	
	Norwich (Trowse)* .... dep.	1	50	
68¼	March	3	17	47¼
		3	20	
88	Spalding	3	45	46¼
		3	47	
126¼	Lincoln.......................................	4	34	48¼
		4	37	
163	Doncaster, tickets	5	23	48
	station	5	25	

* This is the "seaside express" taken after Norwich, where the Yarmouth and Lowestoft portions unite. For uniformity of very high speed this is one of our finest trains.

Journey-speed = 45¼.   Running-average = 47¼.

Now we come to the great lines connecting London with Lancashire and Yorkshire. Here we are in an atmosphere of expresses, and the pitch is raised. On the *Great Northern*, *Midland*, and *North Western* we have performances excellent all round; speed and punctuality become objects of hearty attachment, slow trains are in a minority, carriages are very good, fares low, and all expresses third class.*

Of these three great lines, the Great Northern and Midland rank far above the North Western, not in number of expresses but in speed. The running totals are—

Extent of System in Miles.		Miles.		Running-Average.
635	Great Northern	6,780	at	46¼
1,260	Midland	8,860	,,	45
1,773	North Western	10,400	,,	43$\frac{1}{10}$

* Except the *Irish* mails, which are first and second express fares, and the two nine-hour expresses between King's Cross and Edinburgh, which are first and second ordinary.

but as the North Western is much the most level of the three, the superiority of the other two is greater than the figures indicate. Between the Midland and Great Northern, considering the steep gradients of the former, it might be difficult to apportion merit; but the Great Northern has long been regarded as the fugleman in matters of speed, because what it undertakes to do on paper it does on the metals with exemplary punctuality. At present it is running within itself, for in the year 1880, during the summer months, it ran four trains between Leeds and King's Cross in $3\frac{3}{4}$ hours, a *journey-speed* of $49\frac{1}{2}$.

The Great Northern is a comparatively small line, and not only heads the list for speed, but, in proportion to its length and the population served, provides many more expresses than any other company. The rest of the world outside England cannot show so much high speed.*

GREAT NORTHERN.

The primary expresses run by this line are—

a. 14 for *Manchester* (4 of which are very fast, $4\frac{1}{2}$ hours).
b. 9 „ *Scotland* (see p. 98).
c. 7 „ *Leeds* itself.
d. 3 „ *York* itself.
e. 7 „ *Cambridge* [one more (Down) added November, 1883, 3 P.M.].

but some of these bifurcate, at *Grantham* for Nottingham and Lincoln, and at *Retford* or *Doncaster* for Leeds, York, Hull, giving rise to secondary expresses. Most of the G.N. trains are very long,† but they are run at very high speed with unusual punctuality. The specimen expresses are—

(1.) The 4 best *Manchester* trains (see p. 89)   r.a. $= 50\frac{2}{3}$
(2.) The 1.15 down to *York* (p. 85)   „ $= 49\frac{1}{4}$
(3.) The 9 A.M. up from *Leeds* (4 hours — 5 stops) „ $= 49$
(4.) The "*Scotchman*" (p. 93), (1 stop)   „ $= 49\frac{1}{4}$

* The length given in the preceding page, 635 miles, is not inclusive of *Joint* lines, because the G.N. takes no part in the express running over the joint lines.

† Except the Cambridge and the 4 quick Manchester trains; but these last often run under their time.

Distinct Expresses.

Miles.	Between	Number.	Average: Time. H. M.	Average: Journey-Speed.	Average: Minutes Stopped.	Average: Running-Average.
138½	King's Cross and Retford (*Manchester* and *Leeds* trains)	10	3 6½	44½	10	47
47	Retford and Leeds	5 (3 up)	1 11	40	7	44
185½	King's Cross and Leeds	7 (4 up)	4 18	43	19	46½
32	Doncaster and York	4 (1 up)	– 47	41	5	45¾
105½	King's Cross and Grantham (new *Manchester* expresses)	4	2 5	50⅝	–	50⅝
188	King's Cross and York (*Scotch* expresses)	9 (5 up)*	4 14¾	44¼	12¼	46½
188	King's Cross and York only	3 (2 up)	4 24	42¾	20	46⅕
90	Nottingham and York† ...	2	2 15	40	12	44
127¾	„ King's Cross (8.12 up)	1	2 52	44½	12	48
22¼	Nottingham and Grantham	11 (6 up)	– 31	43	–½	43⅘
24¾	Lincoln and Grantham ...	4	– 36	41¼	2	43⅔
58	Cambridge and King's Cross (one added Nov., 1883)	7 (5 up)	1 21½	42⅔	4	45
		48 chief	averaging	43½	and	46¾ (Mileage 6,307)
		19 auxiliary	„	42⅙	„	44¼ (Mileage 472)
	Total	67	averaging	43	and	46½ (Mileage 6,780)

* The 8 P.M. from King's Cross is not reckoned, as it only runs for a month.
† In summer only.

Service to Chief Towns.

Miles.	Between London and	Number.	Average: Time. H. M.	Average: Journey-Speed.	Average: Minutes Stopped.	Average: Running-Average.
237½	Liverpool	5 (2 up)	5 59	39⅗	39	44½
203	Manchester	14	4 51	41⅚	20	45
199¾	Stockport	7 (3 up)	5 3	39½	31	44
199½*	Halifax	7 (2 „)	4 53½	40¾	28	45
197	Hull	3 (1 „)	4 56	40	31	44⅔
193 *	Bradford	9 (4 „)	4 35	42	25	46⅓
188	York	19 (9 „)	4 20	43⅖	17	46⅗
185½	Leeds......................	13 (7 „)	4 21	42⅔	20½	46¼
162	Sheffield	17 (8 „)	3 39½	44⅓	13	47
156	Doncaster	21 (9 „)	3 35	43½	14½	46⅔
130¼	Lincoln	6 (2 „)	3 11	41	22	46¼
127¾	Nottingham	19 (10 „)	3 0½	42½	15½	46½
105½	Grantham...............	36 (19 „)	2 17½	46	5	47¾
76¼	Peterborough	29 (16 „)	1 37	47	2	48⅙
58	Cambridge	7 (5 „)	1 21½	42⅔	4	45 †

* **Average distance.**
† ***Cambridge*** **is peculiarly well served for its size and importance. See Table IX.**

Long Runs.—There are forty-nine, averaging $73\frac{3}{4}$ miles, at 50 running-average :—

Longest—

		Miles.	H. M.	r.a.	
Grantham and King's Cross		$105\frac{1}{2}$ in 2	4	=51	(2 up *Manch.* exp.)

Quickest—

Grantham to Doncaster.... $50\frac{1}{2}$ in - 58=$52\frac{1}{4}$ (1.15 down)*

7	King's Cross and Grantham	3	Hitchin and Peterborough
1	Grantham and Finsbury Park	1	Sandy and Finsbury Park
4	„ York	5	Doncaster and Grantham
6	King's Cross and Peterborough	2	Retford and York
18	Finsbury Park and Peterborough	1	York and Newark
1	Huntingdon and Finsbury Park	—	
		49	

Express Mileage.—Sixty-seven expresses run 6,780 miles at $46\frac{1}{2}$ running-average (500 miles of which is on very steep gradients north of Wakefield).

Gradients.—The gradients of the three chief lines may be briefly compared. The Great Northern, ending in the latitude of Leeds, escapes the severe gradients which the Midland and North Western encounter in the Westmoreland hills. But, reckoning south of these hills, the *North Western* from Euston to Liverpool and Manchester is much the easiest route, the chief gradient being $\frac{1}{380}$. The *Great Northern* to York comes second, having long pulls of $\frac{1}{200}$ to $\frac{1}{178}$ between King's Cross and Grantham, though from Grantham to York it is nearly level. The *Midland* has a series of heavy ups and downs between St. Pancras and Leicester, gradients chiefly $\frac{1}{178}$, $\frac{1}{132}$, and $\frac{1}{120}$. From Leicester to Leeds it is very easy (except the loop through Sheffield, see p. 88). The Liverpool and Manchester trains branching off at Derby, however, have long and very steep gradients ($\frac{1}{90}$) over the Peak Forest route, 1,000 feet above sea.

The steep portions of each company's route will be described later on (pp. 106—110), in connection with certain Long Runs done over them.

Here we give the *best express* of each of the three lines for comparison :—

* Also on *Sundays*, the 5.0 P.M. runs from Hitchin to Peterborough, $44\frac{1}{4}$ miles, in 50 minutes, = 53 r.a.

Great Northern. Miles		Time. H. M.	Speed.
—	King's Cross	1 15	
76¼	Peterboro'	2 45	50⅝
		2 48	
105½	Grantham	3 26	46
		3 30	
156	Doncaster	4 28	52¼
		4 33	
174	Selby	4 56	47½
		4 58	
187¾	York, tickets	5 17	43⅘
188	station	5 20	—

Journey-speed = 46
Running-average = 49¼

Midland. Miles.		Time. H. M.	Speed.
—	St. Pancras	10 0	
72¼	Kettering....	11 27	49⅘
		11 31	
124	Nottingham	12 35	48½
		12 41	
164½	Sheffield	1 35	45
		1 40	
204	Leeds	2 30	47⅔

Journey-speed = 45¼
Running-average = 48

North Western. Miles.		Time. H. M.	Speed.
—	Birmingham	7 30	—
3¾	Stechford....	7 38	—
		7 39	
19	Coventry	7 59	45¼
		8 1	
30¼	Rugby	8 17	42⅕
		8 20	
107½	Willesden	9 52	50⅔
		9 55	—
113	Euston........	10 5	—

Journey-speed = 43¾
Running-average = 46⅗

MIDLAND.

This line is remarkable for very high speed in the face of severe gradients. It is also to be admired for the *uniform* excellence and symmetrical running of its trains, the roominess of its carriages, and the energy with which it has developed "through" services. It has opened up "cross-country" (*i.e.*, not to and from *London*) communication more than any other Company, as witness the capital services between Bournemouth, Bath, & Bristol, and Liverpool, Manchester, York, Leeds, Hull, & Newcastle. Its engines have nearly one-third of their time occupied in ascending very steep (for an express) gradients, but they have adapted themselves well to their task. For instance, we may compare the slow speed (about 15 miles an hour) at which the Great Western "Dutchman" emerges from the east end of *Box* tunnel,* after only 2 miles of $\frac{1}{100}$, with the heavy load which the Midland Scotch Express pulls up from near *Settle* to *Blea Moor* tunnel at an average of 37 miles an hour, a continuous ascent of 15 miles $\frac{1}{100}$

* This tunnel (oolite) has long borne the false imputation of being 4 or 5 miles in length. It is only 3,193 yards—the Festiniog is 2¼, the Woodhead and Standedge 3 miles each—but it rises $\frac{1}{100}$ (from west to east), which fact, coupled with the disinclination of broad-gauge engines to go up hill (because they have little extra-normal capacity), is responsible for the error.

(except a mile). The run by this same train from St. Pancras to
Leicester (99 miles in 2 hours 7 minutes), and that by the night
express from Skipton to Carlisle (86¾ miles in 1 hour 55 minutes),
are a credit to English workmanship (see pp. 107, 109).

The Midland expresses between Derby and Manchester give a
journey containing some of the loveliest views in England, and
the panorama seen from the Westmoreland heights at 70 miles an
hour is such as few travellers are aware of.* It is true that in
America or elsewhere we ascend to much greater heights, but
without the ingredient of such speed to set off the sight; in other
countries hills make an end of the speed: in England it is *vice
versá.*

The Midland expresses are particularly noteworthy, because
there are none mediocre. All are about equally well equipped,
and about equally spirited. The *Leeds* expresses *viâ* Melton are
certainly quicker than the rest, but then they are much lighter
trains. The total consists of—

a. 10 *Manchester* and *Liverpool* (1 extra from *Manchester*
only), with tributary portions coming on and off at
Derby or Marple (one more, St. Pancras to Liverpool,
added November, 1883—3.40 p.m.)

b. 9 *Leeds viâ* Melton (and 1 extra from *Sheffield*).

c. 6 *Scotch*, with 4 Lancashire and Yorkshire contingents run
separately.

d. 3 *West of England*, between Derby and Bristol, with
auxiliary portions from Liverpool, &c., Leeds, &c., York,
&c., and Hull.

e. 2 *Buxton* and *Liverpool* trains, for business men.

f. Local expresses between *Leeds* and *Derby*, &c.

Of these the two batches (*a*) and (*b*) are admirable services,
highly creditable to engineers and engine-drivers. The Midland
must be thanked for its "through" carriages. Thus there is no
change between *Bristol* and *Glasgow* or *Edinboro'* or *Newcastle;* or
between Leeds, York, Bradford, &c., and *Bournemouth.*

* In summer time the Midland should run a carriage with projecting glass
sides, and charge cheap fares for factory hands to see the sight there is between
Leeds and Carlisle.

Distinct Expresses.

Miles.	Between	Number.	Average Time. H. M.	Journey-Speed.	Minutes Stopped.	Running-Average.
191¼	St. Pancras and Manchester*	11 (6 up)	4 43¾	40½	25½	44½
91½	Derby and Liverpool	6	2 7	43¼	5½	45
42¾	Marple „	4	1 4	40	4	42¾
204	St. Pancras and Leeds, *viâ* Melton	9 (5 up)	4 34½	44½	17	47½
164½	Sheffield and St. Pancras	1 (up)	3 40	44¾	14	48
307¾—9¾	St. Pancras and Carlisle (*Scotch exp.*)†	6	7 30	41	38	45
112¾	Leeds and Carlisle (*Leeds, Liverpool, Manchester*, to *Scotland*)‡	4	2 54	39	15	42½
62½	Derby and Manchester (*night trains*)	2 (down)	1 34	40	4	41⅔
37¾	Stockport and Liverpool (same trains)	2 „	– 55½	40	4	44
75¾	Derby and Leeds (local)	4 (1 up)	1 53	40	10	44
82½	York and Derby (*for W. of England*)	2	2 –	41¼	8	44
130¾	Bristol and Derby „	3 (1 up)§	3 15	40¼	14	43⅓
40	Milford Junction and Hull	8	– 56	43	2	44⅖
62	Buxton and Liverpool (through trains)	2	1 23½	44½	2	45⅝
128¾	St. Pancras and Derby (12.25 *Buxton*)	1 (down)	3 10	40⅗	18	45
91½	Liverpool and Derby (up *Bristol* exp.)	1	2 15	40⅔	7	43
	Total	66	averaging	41⅗	and	45 (8,860 m.)

* Ten of these serve both Manchester and Liverpool, the Liverpool portion coming on and off at Derby and Marple. The eleventh (up) is from Manchester only.

† Average distance, 308¾ miles.

‡ Mostly hill gradients. The Liverpool and Manchester portions join at *Hellifield*.

§ Two each way, but the other up is not so fast.

Service to Chief Towns.

	Miles.	Between London and	Number.	Average Time. H. M.	Journey-Speed.	Minutes stopped.	r.a.
	*307¾—310	Carlisle	7 (3 up)	7 29½	41¼	40	45¼
	220¼	Liverpool	10	5 21	41⅙	30	45⅗
Old route	209½—211½	Bradford	4	5 5	41⅗	25	45 †
Viâ Melton	217½		9 (5 up)	5 5	42¾	24	46½ †
Old route	196—198	Leeds	6 (2 „)	4 42½	42	21½	45⅓ ‡
Viâ Melton	204		9 (5 „)	4 34½	44½	17	47½ ‡
	191¼	Manchester	11 (6 „)	4 43¾	40½	25½	44⅗
	182½	Stockport	11 (6 „)	4 32	40¼	27	44⅔
Old route	158½	Sheffield	6	3 40⅔	43	14	46 §
Viâ Melton	164½		10 (6 up)	3 40	44⅚	13	47⅗ §
	128¾	Derby	15 (7 „)	3 1½	42⅓	15	46⅝ ‖
Viâ Melton	138½		6	3 21	41	22	46½ ‖
„ Trent	126½	Notting-ham	6 (2 up)	3 –	42⅙	15½	46 ¶
„ Kettering	124		10	2 40	46½	7	48⅔ ¶
	99¼	Leicester	20	2 14	44½	7	47
	49¾	Bedford	17 (9 up)	1 8	44	2½	45½

* Some run *viâ* Sheffield, some *viâ* Staveley and Eckington.

† Thirteen average 46 r.a.

‡ Fifteen average 46⅔ r.a.

§ Sixteen average 47 r.a.

‖ Twenty-one average 46½ r.a.

¶ Sixteen average 47⅔ r.a.

Long Runs.—There are one hundred and four averaging 53 miles, at 46½ running-average (sixteen of these are contingent on picking up and setting down), of which twenty-four average 74 miles at 46¾ running-average, and sixteen average 66 miles at 44 running-average, *over hill gradients* (Derbyshire, Westmoreland, &c.).

10	London and Kettering	2	Marple and Liverpool
10	Kettering and Nottingham	1	Buxton „
9	Nottingham and Sheffield	1	„ Warrington
12	Sheffield and Leeds	1	Derby and Liverpool
5	St. Pancras and Bedford	1	Mill. Dale and Liverpool
9	Kent. Tn. „	4	Saltley and Cheltenham
15	Leicester „	1	Belper and Stockport
2	St. Pancras and Leicester	1	Masborough and York
2	Trent and Normanton	12	in Westmoreland district
1	Leicester and Luton		
2	Marple and Derby		—
3	Stockport and Derby	104	

Longest—   Miles. H. M. r.a.
St. Pancras to Leicester   99¼ in 2   7 = 47 (see p. 107).

Quickest—
St. Pancras to Kettering   72½ „ 1 27 = 49¼ (10.0 down) hilly run.

Liverpool to Stockport   37¾ „ – 45 = 50⅓ { With or without a stoppage.

Skipton to Carlisle ....   86¾ „ 1 55 = 45¼ Very steep (p. 109).

Bedford to Kentish Tn.   48   „ 1 – = 48 { Steep. Run by all the *Manchester* expresses in the hour.

Express Mileage.—Sixty-six expresses run 8,860 miles, at 45 running-average.

Gradients.—Those between St. Pancras and Leicester, and Skipton to Carlisle, will be given in detail later. From Leicester to Leeds is nearly level, except that those trains which run *via Sheffield* have (going north) 5 miles $\frac{1}{100}$ up, and 6 miles $\frac{1}{100}$ down, at the Bradway tunnel. From Leeds to Skipton the line rises easily. The steep piece between Derby and Manchester will be given later.

Weight, &c.—Most of the Midland expresses are very heavy, heavier than appears at first sight, because of the massive construction of their Pullman and ordinary bogies. Their punctuality is not as good as their speed, especially in summer. Engines and drivers are not to blame, for they generally do at least as much as they are timed to do; but the Midland main line is a river with many affluents, and a profusion of "through carriages" involves much waste of time at important stations.

Best Express.—This has already been given with the Great Northern. Here we will take the best express of each of the three lines to *Manchester*, for which town competition is keener than for any other :—

GREAT NORTHERN. (M. S. & L. from Retford to Manch.)

Miles.		Time. H. M.	Speed.
—	Manchester	11 0	40⅓
41	Sheffield ...	12 1	
		12 5	44⅗
97½	Grantham...	1 21	
		1 26	51
203	King's Cross	3 30	

Journey-speed = 45.

Running-average = 46⅔.

Exp. 14 { 2 trains each way like this. 10 others express.

MIDLAND.

Miles.		Time. H. M.	Speed.
—	Manchester (Central)..	3 45	40
31¼	Miller's Dale..	4 32	
		4 35	45¾
62½	Derby	5 16	
		5 21	46⅔
92	Leicester	5 59	
		6 4	48
141½	Bedford	7 6	
		7 10	45
161	Luton	7 36	
		7 37	47½
189½	Kentish Town	8 13	
		8 16	
191¼	St. Pancras ...	8 20	

Journey-speed = 41¾.

Running-average = 45⅙.

Exp. 11 { 2 others (down) take 4 hours 40 minutes. 8 others express.

NORTH WESTERN.

Miles		Time. H. M.	Speed.
—	Manchester ...	11 15	32
4¾	Stockport.......	11 24	
		11 25	38
14	Alderley Edge	11 40	
		11 41	40⅘
31	Crewe	12 6	
		12 15	47½
106¼	Rugby	1 50	
		1 58	49⅓
183½	Willesden ...	3 32	
		3 35	33
189	Euston..........	3 45	

Journey-speed = 42.
Running-average = 45⅔

Exp. 17 { 3 do it in this time (2 up). 2 others (down) take 4 hours 35 minutes. 12 others express.

The log of these three trains is characteristic. There is an heroic simplicity about that of the Great Northern, which, having a route 12 miles the longest and a course not much easier than the hardest of the three, straightway proceeds to do its journey as quick as either. But its trains in this case are comparatively light.

The Midland stops wherever it can absorb passengers, and works very hard the whole way, taking gradients as part of the day's programme. Its trains are the heaviest of the three.

The North Western as usual dallies so much over a small section of the route, that it makes the running-average of the whole run considerably less than it need be. It runs from *Liverpool*, 193½ miles, in the same time, 4½ hours.

NORTH WESTERN.

This is the old established railway firm, and does a larger business than either of its more energetic rivals. Being the first made, it has easier gradients, and has had a longer time to form trade connections. Its route is also the shortest to many of our busiest towns. For these reasons it is much the wealthiest of our great companies, and probably earns its revenue more easily. But, from an express point of view, it is slack compared with the Great Northern or Midland; it runs more expresses, only at a lower speed. This is partly because competition merely requires it to serve towns in the same time as the other two lines; and, being generally on the short route, it need not run so fast. Also its main line is so thronged with fast trains, that any acceleration, affecting such a number, is more tardily proposed. Running so many expresses on one main line (south of Crewe), its punctuality and discipline are first class, and hence accidents are very uncommon. Its trains are often very long ones, but are not so heavy in proportion to length as on the Midland or Great Northern.

The express service of the North Western to *Liverpool* and *Birmingham* is considerably spoilt by the waiting at Crewe and Rugby of several trains, and by the slow running on the parts between Crewe and Liverpool and Rugby and Birmingham. Thus, though Manchester has 17 London expresses, Liverpool has only 10, in spite of the North Western being the direct thoroughfare from London to America. Birmingham has but 8 London trains which can possibly be called express, though between Rugby (which is only 30 miles off) and Euston there are fifty. In fact, *Birmingham* is, for its size, very poorly served, having a total (North Western and Great Western) of 12 against 28 for *Leeds*, which is so much farther away. *Liverpool*, too, cannot boast of obtaining its due speed from the North Western; it is the same distance from Euston as Exeter from Paddington, but its fastest train is 16 minutes longer than the "Dutchman" (which latter stops more on the journey).

There is *no express service* between two such important towns as *Manchester* and *Leeds* ($42\frac{3}{4}$ miles); the two quickest take 1 hour 20 minutes, a journey-speed of only 32, which compares badly with that of the M.S. & L. between Manchester and Sheffield, over twice the obstacles (see p. 96).

The *Irish Mail* Service, of which the North Western has the monopoly, is not much credit to the Company. These trains are limited to 1st and 2nd class at express fares, and yet are the slowest of any of the expresses run to an important place. The "running-average" of the quickest (7.15 down) is only $43\frac{2}{3}$, and the running-average of the four trains only $42\frac{1}{4}$. The acceleration of *half an hour* lately promised to the Government will hardly raise the "journey-speed" to 44, a speed very good, but lower than that which Leeds and Manchester obtain without a premium from Government.

The smartest running of the North Western is that of its twenty expresses on the old line between Liverpool and Manchester, and two of its up expresses from Birmingham; the former, over a short course, have a running-average of 48, and the latter exceed 50 between Rugby and Willesden.

Distinct Expresses.

Miles.	Between	Number.	Average: Time. H.	M.	Journey-Speed.	Minutes Stopped.	Running-Average.	
31½	Liverpool and Manchester (Vict.) (1 goes to *Lond. Road* in 50 min.)	20	–	45	42	3	45*	
182½–191	Euston and Manchester (the 16 trains average 188·9 miles)	16	4	43	40	24½	43⅘	
193½	Euston and Livpool. only	2 (up)	4	30	43	17	46	
35½	Crewe "	5 (3 up)	–	55	38¾†	4	41⅘	
60	Stafford "	3 (1 ")	1	35	38†	9	42⁶⁄₇	
299¼	Euston and Carlisle (*Scotch* expresses)	7 (4 up)	7	28½‡	40	34½	43⅓	
263¾—5¾	Euston and Holyhead (*Irish Mail*) (1 *viâ* Northampton; the 4 average 264½)	4	6	42½	39½	24	42	
113—115	Euston and Birmingham (5 *viâ* Northampton; the 7 average 114½)	7 (3 up)	2	46	41⅜	13	45	
158—160	Euston and Crewe (3 *viâ* Northampton)	7 (2 up)	3	57	40¼	20	44	
82¾—84¾	Euston and Rugby (average 84 miles)	8§	2	3½	40⅝	7	43¼	
90	Preston & Carlisle (trains from *Liverpool & Manchester* to Scotland)	3 (2 up)‖	2	13	40⅝	6	42¼	
								Mileage.
	Total	54 chief,	averaging		40½	and	43⅜	9,418
		28 auxiliary,	"		41	"	44	987
		82	averaging		40⅜	and	43⁷⁄₁₀	10,405

* The running-average is 48 when clear of the Edge Hill Tunnel.

† Only admitted through the excuse of Edge Hill Tunnel.

‡ Two others up average 7¾ hours = 38⅝ journey-speed, but not admitted because the proportion of hilly route to such a long journey is not enough to excuse the speed. The 7.30 P.M. from Euston is not counted, as it only runs a short time.

§ These are really main line residues of trains which are meant for express to Liverpool and Manchester or Birmingham.

‖ Giving, with the seven other Scotch expresses, a total of ten expresses between Preston and Carlisle.

Service to Chief Towns.

Miles.*	Between London and	Number.	Average			
			Time.	Journey-Speed.	Minutes Stopped.	r.a.
			H. M.			
299¼	Carlisle	7 (4 up)	7 28½	40	34½	43⅓
209¼	Preston	8	5 6	41	24	44½
193½—195½	Liverpool (3 *viâ* Northm)...	10 (6 up)	4 45	40$\frac{6}{7}$	25	44¾
182½—191	Manchester	17 (8 „)	4 46	39⅔	24½	43⅓†
177 —185½	Stockport	„	10m. less	—	—	—
182¼—184¼	Warrington (2 *viâ* Northm)	12	4 33	40	26	44¼
179	Chester (1 *viâ* Northm)	9 (4 up)	4 25	40⅗	21	44
163	Shrewsbury	3 (1 „)	4 3	40¼	24	44⅗
158—160	Crewe (4 *viâ* Northm)	34 (16 „)	3 48	41⅗	15½	44⅗
113—115	Birmingham (5 *viâ* Northm)	8	2 45½	41⅖	12⅓	44¾
82¾—84¾	Rugby (21 *viâ* Northm.) Av. distance 83⅓ miles	50	1 57	42	5	44⅘
65¾	Northampton	21 (9 up)	1 32	43	4	44⅘

* The North Western distances are varied by many of the trains running on the Northampton Loop instead of *viâ* Kilsby Tunnel. This makes the run two miles longer. In the case of Manchester, trains run either *viâ* Crewe, 189 miles, or *viâ* Stafford and Norton Bridge, 186½ miles, or *viâ* Rugeley Junction and Stone, 182½ miles; and any of these trains running *viâ* Northampton has two miles extra; thus the Manchester distances vary from 191 to 182½ miles.

† 13 trains run *viâ* Crewe and 5 of these *viâ* Northampton.
3 „ Stafford and 1 of these *viâ* Northampton.
1 „ Colwich.
The average distance is 189 miles.

Long Runs.—There are ninety-eight, averaging 60 miles, at 45 running-average (this is really more long runs than the *Midland*, because several of the latter are contingent on signal to pick up or set down), of which fifty-three (over 60 miles) average 72 miles at 44 running-average, and twelve, *over Westmoreland hills*, average 60¾ miles, at 43 running-average.

1 Euston and Nuneaton	6 Crewe and Nuneaton
2 „ Rugby	2 „ Preston
13 Willesden and „	9 Rugby and Stafford
11 „ Northampton	1 „ Leighton
20 „ Bletchley	1 Bletchley and Euston
1 Euston and Northampton	1 Chester and Stafford
1 Rugby and Watford	5 „ Holyhead
1 Willesden and Roade	2 „ Bangor
1 „ Weedon	12 over Westmoreland hills
1 „ Blisworth	—
7 Crewe and Rugby	98

Longest—

	Miles.		H. M.		r.a.	
Nuneaton to Willesden	91⅓	in	1 57	=	47	(up day Scotch express)

Quickest—

Northampton to Willesden	60¼	„	1 10	=	51⅗	(9.30 up from Birmgm.)
Rugby to Willesden	77¼	„	1 32	=	50⅓	(7.30 „)
Carlisle to Carnforth (over 915 feet)	62¾	„	1 25	=	44¼	(night mail)

Best Express.—This has been already given with the Great Northern. Here we will take the best *Scotch* express of each of the three great lines :—

East Coast Route.

Miles		Time. A.M.	Speed
—	Glasgow....dep.	8 40	—
1½	Cowlairs	8 46 / 8 48	—
25	Polmont Jntn.	9 19 / 9 20	45½
46	Haymarket	9 50 / 9 52	42
47¼	Edinb.(Wav.)	9 55 / 10 —	
104¾	Berwick	11 15 / 11 20	46
171½	Newcastle	12 45 / 12 50	47
207½	Darlington	1 38 / 1 41	45
251¼	York (*refreshments*)	2 35 / 3 5	49½
334¼	Grantham	4 44 / 4 50	50
439¾	King's Cross	7 —	48½

(for *Gradients*, see pp. 100 & 106)

Midland Route.

Miles		Time. A.M.	Speed
—	St. Pancras dep	10 35	47
99¼	Leicester	12 42 / 12 46	
120	Trent	1 14 / 1 17	44½
185¼	Normanton (*refreshments*)	2 40 / 3 10	47
221½	Skipton	4 2 / 4 5	41½
277½	Appleby	5 21 / 5 24	44½
307¾	Carlisle ....arr.	6 5	44½
„	dep.	6 12	42½
353¼	Hawick	7 16 / 7 17	
369	Melrose	7 41 / 7 42	39
372½	Galashiels	7 49 / 7 52	
406	Edinburgh	8 42	40½
—	Carlisle....dep.	6 12	47
340¾	Dumfries	6 54 / 6 57	
399¼	Kilmarnock	8 17 / 8 20	44¾
423	Glasgow	8 55	40¾

(*Gradients* pp. 88, 107, 109, 108, 101)

West Coast Route.

Miles		Time. A.M.	Speed
—	Euston ..... dep.	10 —	
5½	Willesden	10 9 / 10 12	
82¾	Rugby	11 55 / 12 —	45
158	Crewe	1 36 / 1 43	47
209¼	Preston (*refreshments*)	2 50 / 3 10	46
299¼	Carlisle	5 20 / 5 28	41½
339	Beattock	6 16 / 6 19	49¾
372¾	Carstairs ....arr.	7 4	45
„	dep.	7 7	
400¼	{ Edinb. tick. station }	7 47 / 7 50	41¼
—	Carstairs dep.	7 6	
383½	Law Junction	7 21 / 7 23	39
400½	Glasgow, Egl. St.	7 56	31
401½	„ Central	8 —	

(*Gradients* pp. 109 and 110)

j.s. = 42½ } from Glasgow.
r.a. = 47
j.s. = 43¾ } „ Edinburgh.
r.a. = 48

The *North British* Company work these trains between Glasgow and Edinburgh; the *North Eastern* between Edinburgh and York; and the *Great Northern* York and London.

j.s. = 40 1/10 } to Glasgow.
r.a. = 45
j.s. = 40½ } „ Edinburgh
r.a. = 44½ } (much steeper).

The *Midland* work as far as Carlisle, from which the *North British* take the Edinburgh and the *Glasgow and South Western* the Glasgow portions.

j.s. = 40½ } to Glasgow.
r.a. = 44
j.s. = 40¾ } „ Edinburgh.
r.a. = 44¾

Worked by the *North Western* to Carlisle, and by the *Caledonian* beyond. This latter Company mounts the hill of 1,015 feet between Beattock and Carstairs at a very good speed indeed.

Of these three journeys, speaking roughly, the *Midland* has the severest route, rising to 1,170 feet in Westmoreland, and in the

Lowlands to 950 and 850 feet respectively, with a drop of 600 feet between. The *North Western* is considerably easier, chiefly from the gentle gradients south of Preston; it rises to 915 feet in Westmoreland, and 1,015 and 880 feet in the Lowlands, with a drop of 250 feet between. The East coast route is never so high as 400 feet (360 feet at *Knebworth*, Herts, and 380 at *Grant's House*, north of Berwick).

While we are examining Scotch expresses, we may, in passing, compare the *Limited mail* of the *North Western*, by no means one of our very best trains, with the very best *long distance* train on the Continent, that of the *Paris, Lyon, & Mediterranée.* The English train is third class; the French one "first only:"—

Miles.		Time.	Speed.
		P. M.	
—	Euston, dep.	8 50	45
82¾	Rugby	10 40	
		10 44	45
110	Tamworth	11 20	
		11 24	45½
133½	Stafford	11 55	
		11 59	44⅔
158	Crewe	12 32	
		12 38	46¾
194	Wigan	1 24	
		1 30	40
209¼	Preston	1 53	
		1 57	40⅜
299¼	Carlisle	4 10	
		4 18	48½*
372¾	Carstairs	5 53	
		6 –	36
389	Holytown Junction	6 27	
		6 29	
393½	Coatbridge	6 37	—
		6 40	
409	Larbert	7 3	40½
		7 7	
417¼	Stirling	7 21	
		7 24	—
450½	Perth .... Tickets	8 13	
	station	8 15	40
	" dep.	9 5	
482¾	Forfar	9 55	39½
		9 59	
498¼	Bridge of Dun	10 28	32
		10 29	
540¼	ABERDEEN Tickets	11 37	37
	station	11 40	

Journey-speed = 36⅝.
Running-average = 41⅛.

Miles.		Time.	Speed.
		A. M.	
—	Paris†	8 55	
			36
49	Montereau	10 17	
		10 20	
			41½
96½	Laroche	11 28	
		11 31	
			41¾
122¼	Tonnerre	12 8	
		12 33	
			39½
195½	Dijon	2 24	
		2 29	
			42
273¾	Macon	4 21	
		4 26	
			34½
314¾	Lyon	5 37	
		6 8	
			40
383¾	Valence	7 51	
		7 56	
			42½
460¾	Avignon	9 45	
		9 50	
			38⅞
536	Marseilles	11 47	

Journey-speed = 36.
Running-average = 39⅞.

* There is a stop at the summit of ascent for four minutes. Beattock is 350 feet above sea, and the summit 1,015 feet; gradients chiefly about $\frac{1}{80}$.

† This was the train last winter; it is not running now, but a slower one later in the day (7.15 p.m.).

This comparison merely illustrates the energy with which our trains are managed in England. The journey to Aberdeen does not pretend to be express, as the train is a heavy mail, which is continually picking up letters; secondly, this train stops at Perth (the mail bags go on alone to Aberdeen ahead of passengers), and there is a pause of fifty minutes before the Aberdeen portion starts; thirdly, there are two severe pieces of gradient on the way, one up to 915 feet at Shap, the other 1,015 feet north of Beattock.

Yet this mail, with the stop at Perth, casually affords a finer express run than the French train, which is a light one, has an easier route, stops 8 times and 82 minutes as against 15 times and 114 minutes, and is run as a special express at special first class fares.

This Marseilles express, though admirable for the series of very long breaks in its running, is very poor in result, compared with what, *e.g.*, the Great Northern would do if it had such an opening. There are, however, *quicker* trains in France. We give the quickest, which is also much the fastest on the Continent:—

"*First Class only.*"

Miles.		Time.	Speed.
		A. M.	
	Bordeaux (Bastide) .... dep.	7 50	
21¾	Libourne	8 21	42
		8 23	
31¾	Coutras	8 39	37½
		8 41	
82¾	Angoulême	9 50	44⅓
		10 15	
112	Ruffec	10 56	42⅘
		10 59	
153	Poitiers	11 55	44
		12 0	
173¼	Châtellerault	12 30	40½
		12 32	
215½	St. Pierre des Corps	1 30	43¾
		1 35	
248½	Blois	2 20	44
		2 22	
285	Les Aubrais	3 10	45⅔
		3 15	
324¼	Etampes	4 7	45⅓
		4 10	
359	Paris	4 56	45⅓

Journey-speed = 39½. Running-average = 43¾.

In the United States, from the absence of anything corresponding to our "Bradshaw," it is difficult to collect the prevalent speeds at which journeys are accomplished. But we think it is safe to say that the entire States cannot show an amount of high speed equal to that on the Great Northern alone in England. The one or two few really fine bits of running are done on the Reading line, between New York and Philadelphia, where the track is straight and nearly level. (Some of these runs average 49 r.a.)

Having disposed of the great lines, we come next to a working partner of one of them, the—

MANCHESTER, SHEFFIELD, AND LINCOLN.

This little line has two sets of expresses, both equally a credit to it, though they may not appear so in figures—

(a.) It takes the carriages of the *Great Northern* Manchester and Liverpool trains along with its own from Retford to Manchester, parting at Penistone or Godley for Liverpool.

(b.) It runs thirty-two admirable trains between Liverpool and Manchester, on the new line built by the joint committee of the Manchester, Sheffield, and Lincoln, Great Northern, and Midland Railways.

None of these are very heavy trains, and their punctuality is excellent.

Gradients.—(a.) This is a route to breed energy. Of the $64\frac{1}{2}$ miles from Retford to Manchester, 7 only are easier than $\frac{1}{300}$; the other 56 average $\frac{1}{140}$. On such a route a journey speed of 35 would be express. From *Retford* it rises $3\frac{1}{2}$ miles averaging $\frac{1}{100}$; falls 3 more gently to *Worksop;* rises (two rests) 7 miles averaging $\frac{1}{140}$, and falls $3\frac{1}{2}$ miles averaging $\frac{1}{140}$ to *Woodhouse Junction;* rises 3 miles $\frac{1}{115}$ to *Handsworth* tunnel, and falls $2\frac{1}{2}$ miles averaging $\frac{1}{110}$ into *Sheffield.*

From *Sheffield* to *Manchester* it resembles the roof of a house 18½ miles of unbroken ascent averaging $\frac{1}{125}$ to the east mouth of the *Woodhead* tunnel, 1,010 feet, followed by a drop of $22\frac{1}{2}$ miles averaging $\frac{1}{145}$ (3 easy) to Manchester.

(b.) This line is mostly easy. Of the 18 miles between *Liverpool* and *Warrington*, 9 are $\frac{1}{500}$ or $\frac{1}{135}$, short undulations; of the 16 miles from *Warrington* to *Manchester* 14 are practically level.

The gradients of the rival line ("High Level" L. & N.W.), that made by Stephenson in 1830, are as follows:—a mile of $\frac{1}{97}$ up out of Lime Street to *Edge Hill*, $1\frac{1}{4}$ mile of $\frac{1}{97}$ up before *Rainhill*, 1 mile of $\frac{1}{89}$ down before *St. Helen's Jn.*, a mile of $\frac{1}{103}$ up into Manchester (Vict.); the rest of the $31\frac{1}{2}$ miles are practically level.

Distinct Expresses.

Miles.	Between	Number.	Average			
			Time.	Journey-Speed.	Minutes Stopped.	Running-Average.
$64\frac{1}{4}$	Retford and Manchester....	10	H. M. 1 46½	36½	10	40 *
$62\frac{1}{4}$	Penistone and Liverpool	3 (2 up)	1 41	37	12	42
$97\frac{1}{4}$	Manchester and Grantham	4	2 20	41½	5	43¾†
$34\frac{1}{4}$ {	Liverpool and Manchester	28	– 45	45¾	2	47¾‡
	„	4	– 40	51⅓	—	51¾‡
	Total	49	averaging	43	and	Mileage. 44¾ 2,318

* Great Northern ordinary expresses.   † Great Northern 4¼ hour expresses.
‡ Thirty-two, averaging 48¼ running-average.

Service for Chief Towns.—The service between Manchester, Liverpool, Sheffield, and *London*, has been already given under the Great Northern. That between *Liverpool and Manchester themselves* is by far the best service in England. Fast trains began here, and here we find them at their best. Between these two towns we have—

Trains.

32 M. S & L., averaging 44½ minutes, with a r.a. of 48¼*
†20 L. & N.W.   „   45   „   47¾‡

Total 52 expresses, with a running-average of 48.

There are not many deaths of *ennui* in this neighbourhood. Until last summer the Midland contributed sixteen more expresses between the towns, averaging 48 running-average as well; but its trains between *Liverpool* and London now run *viâ* Stockport and Warrington; also between *Warrington* and Liverpool there come in the five G. Northern Liverpool expresses. Besides these there

* The twenty-eight ¾-hour trains of the Manchester, Sheffield, and Lincoln start from each end at the half-past, from 8½ a.m. to 9½ p.m. The ¾-hr. trains of the London and North Western start from each end at the hour, from 9 a.m. to 8 p.m. [there are only 20 that run in ¾-hr., the other 4 take 50 minutes].
† One of these runs to London Road, in 50 minutes (37¾ miles).
‡ Excluding Edge Hill tunnel, 1¼ miles, which consumes about five minutes.

are about two dozen trains that are only slower because they make more stops; thus the North Western has 13, averaging 55¾ minutes, between Manchester and Liverpool. (There are in all four lines for the two towns, one "low level" North Western, *viâ* Warrington, and another *viâ* Wigan, in addition to the two on which expresses run.)

Long Runs of the *Manchester, Sheffield, and Lincoln.*—There are 8 averaging 48¾ miles, at 43½ running-average (the quick *Gt. Northern* trains), over a course of nothing but steep gradients. The *Longest* are between Sheffield and Grantham, 56¼ miles, in 1 hour 12 minutes = 47 running-average. *Quickest*, Manchester to Warrington, 16 miles, in 18 minutes = 53⅓ running-average (done sixteen times daily).

Express Mileage.—Forty-nine expresses run 2,318 miles, at 44⅘ running-average.

There are four lines left, whose express running consists almost entirely of the part they take in working the *Scotch* trains of the three great companies. These are the *North Eastern* and the Scotch lines, *North British, Caledonian, Glasgow & South Western.*

NORTH EASTERN.

This is a line more noted for dividends than expresses. It is a very easy line for fast running, but makes little use of its opportunities. Of ten trains [9 strictly "*Scotch*" and 1 *Newspaper*, see p. 83] which the Great Northern does its best to make "express" for Edinburgh, the North Eastern forwards four (5.15 down, 10.15, 12.40, and 7.30 up from Edinburgh) so moderately that they fail to be express on the whole journey. Thus there are six instead of ten "Scotch" expresses between Edinburgh and King's Cross. The other express trains of the North Eastern are scanty and disappointing, considering the generally easy track; those to Scarborough are perhaps the most brisk, but the running-average of these is low because of a series of sharp curves beside the *Derwent* near Malton, which necessitate quiet running. Many of the towns on the North Eastern system, *e.g., Sunderland, Stockton,*

Middlesborough, are badly off for express communication. This is owing to the crooked network of little parochial lines which early grew up in Durham, so that now there is great lack of straight through routes.

On the other hand, if the North Eastern cannot boast much real "express" speed, it runs a large number of trains that are high in the second rank, brisk and smart in the midst of stoppages. It is by tradition and feeling a very *local* line, [railways began at *Darlington*, now the centre of the N. Eastern system] and as, in addition, a great part of its routes lie through districts studded with collieries, furnaces, busy works, and large towns, it is often impracticable to have long breaks of high speed.

Too much praise cannot be given this Company for the comfortable equipment of its trains. Serving a part of England where the best "democratic" mood prevails, it has caught the spirit of its surroundings, and provides the public with *third-class carriages* so inviting in appearance that even a flunkey, entering by mistake, has been known to travel from York to Newcastle without loss of respectability. The North Eastern also holds a place of honour in regard to *brakes;* almost every train on a small branch has the Westinghouse automatic. Lastly, its *return fares* are the lowest in the country.

The main-line expresses are some of the very longest and heaviest in England, and rarely lose time on their own section; but they often consume more time than is allotted them for stops at *Darlington* or *Newcastle :* in the first case because of the insufficient platform area, in the second from the awkward position of the station. Many of the engines will not start without "jibbing."

The North Eastern is the Company owning more romantic and beautiful views than any other. These abound either on the seacoast from Flamborough to Berwick, or along the valleys by which it makes three passages through the Pennine, 1st, from Newcastle to Carlisle; 2nd, from Northallerton to Hawes; 3rd, from Darlington to Penrith. On this latter journey, between *Bowes* and *Barras*, the line mounts up [gradients $\frac{1}{85}$ to $\frac{1}{75}$] to 1,369 feet above sea on Stainmoor, where it crosses the boundary of Yorkshire and Westmoreland. This is the highest passenger route in England.

Gradients.—The North Eastern Railway begins at *Shaftholme*, 4 miles north of Doncaster, and ends at *Berwick*, 175 miles. Of these 175 miles about 100 are easier than $\frac{1}{500}$, 37 are from $\frac{1}{500}$ to $\frac{1}{110}$, and 37 between $\frac{1}{110}$ and $\frac{1}{115}$ ($\frac{1}{160}$ and $\frac{1}{200}$ most common). The first 70 miles, as far north as *Darlington*, are practically level. Here then is the place for speed, but except in the case of the two 9-hour Scotch trains, it is by no means the fact.

The North Eastern also works the through Scotch trains over the *North British* between Berwick and Edinburgh. The gradients here are much harder. From Berwick the line rises off and on 17 miles (9 of which in two ascents are $\frac{1}{200}$) to near *Grant's House*, 380 feet; from this it drops 4½ miles of $\frac{1}{96}$ and 1½ of $\frac{1}{310}$ to *Innerwick*, and then proceeds 33 miles with easy undulations (mostly $\frac{1}{300}$) to *St. Margaret's*, from which it mounts 1¼ miles of $\frac{1}{75}$ to Edinburgh.

Distinct Expresses.

Miles.	Between	Number.	Average			
			Time.	Journey-Speed.	Minutes Stopped.	Running-Average.
			H. M.			
204¼	York and Edinburgh ⌈Scotch	6 (2 up)	4 58½	41	18	43¾
147	„ Berwick.... ⌊ trains	1 down	3 43	40	14	42½†
80¼*	Newcastle and York	5 (3 up)	2 –	40	9¼	43½
54	Hull and Leeds	3	1 18	41½	5	44¾
42¾	York and Scarborough	4	1 5¼	39	1½	40
						Mileage.
	Total	19	averaging	40½	and	43¼ 2,112

* This distance is often given as 83¼ miles, because until lately the Companies charged as for three additional miles as a toll for crossing the High Level bridge at Newcastle; thus Edinburgh was made to appear 395¼ miles from King's Cross, instead of 392¼.

† 9 P.M. from King's Cross, not express beyond Berwick or between King's Cross and York.

London Service of Chief Towns.

Miles.	Between London and	Number.	Average			
			Time.	Journey-Speed.	Minutes Stopped.	Running-Average.
			H. M.			
335	Berwick.....................	6 (2 up)	8 1	41¾	· 42	45¼
268½	Newcastle	10	6 28½	41½	38	46
254	Durham	8 (5 up)	6 18	40¾	40	45
(244½	Whitby.....................	2	6 32½	37½	41¼	41¾*)
232¼	Darlington	11 (7 up)	5 43	40¾	38	45½
230¾	Scarborough............	8	5 42¼	40¼	40¼	45⅝

* May be admitted, because of the exceptional curves and gradients between Pickering and Whitby.

Long Runs.—There are twenty, averaging 56 miles, at 44¾ running-average. *Longest*, York to Newcastle, 80¼ miles, in 1 hour

42 minutes = 47⅓ running-average. *Quickest*, York to Darlington, 44¼ miles, in 53 minutes = 50 running-average (3.25 from York).

2 York and Newcastle	1 Berwick and Drem Junction
6 Newcastle and Berwick	2 York and Scarborough
6 York and Darlington	—
3 Berwick and Edinburgh	20

Express Mileage.—Nineteen expresses run 2,110 miles at 43¼ running-average.

SCOTCH LINES.

There are three Scotch Companies that run expresses, and they do this over a course beset with gradients. The *Glasgow & South Western* take the Midland carriages between Glasgow and Carlisle; the *Caledonian* work the North Western trains between Glasgow, Edinburgh, Perth, and Carlisle; while the *North British* run Midland expresses between Edinburgh and Carlisle; and the Great Northern expresses worked by the North Eastern come over its main line from Berwick to Edinburgh. The North British and Caledonian have also local expresses between Edinburgh and Glasgow.

Of these three lines the express running is in each case very good, as any experience of either will attest. And though, owing to the steep ascents of unusual length, the running-average is low compared with southern lines, yet here the man who wishes to see what 70 miles an hour means can readily be satisfied, and nowhere better than here may he see how little compensatory effect a speed of 70 miles an hour *down* such a hill as $\frac{1}{75}$ can have in making good the loss of time going *up* the other side.

The Glasgow & South Western is a much gentler route than the other two. The gradients of the former we now give—of the other two a little later.

Gradients. Glasgow and South Western.—From Carlisle the line falls gently 7 miles, rises 3 miles $\frac{1}{800}$ to *Gretna*, runs 13 miles nearly level, undulates $\frac{1}{800}$ for 5 miles, followed by 10 miles nearly level; then a long ascent with the *River Nith* for 35 miles (12 are about $\frac{1}{150}$ to $\frac{1}{100}$, the rest easy) to *New Cumnock*, 625 feet above sea. It then falls 18 miles (mostly $\frac{1}{100}$ to $\frac{1}{150}$, 3 miles nearly level) to *Kilmarnock*, 140 feet. From here the *express* route mounts

7 miles very steeply ($\frac{1}{75}$ to $\frac{1}{150}$), falls gently 5 miles to *Caldwell*, drops steeply 4½ miles $\frac{1}{70}$ to *Barrhead*, and falls 7 miles more gently into Glasgow, 115 miles. (The old route runs from Kilmarnock round *viâ* Paisley, nearly level, but 10 miles longer.)

Distinct Expresses of the Three Scotch Companies.

Company.	Miles.	Between	Number.	Average				Express Mileage.
				Time.	Journey-Speed.	Minutes Stopped.	r.a.	
				H. M.				Miles.
G. & S.W	115¼	Glasgow and Carlisle	8	2 46	41⅔	7	43⅓	922
N. BRIT.	47¼	Glasgow and Edinburgh ..	5 (3 up)	1 14	38⅓	5	41*	—
	98¼	Carlisle and Edinburgh....	6	2 29	39½	5	41	—
			11	averaging	39	and	41	825
CALEDONIAN	102	Glasgow and Carlisle	2	2 36	39¼	13	42⅘	—
	101¼	Edinburgh and Carlisle...	7 (3 up)	2 30¾	40	10	43	—
	45¼	Edinburgh and Glasgow .. (Egl. St.), *viâ* Midcalder	4	1 8½	40	3	41½	—
	20¾	Dundee and Perth	3 (1 up)	– 30	41½	—	41½	—
			16	averaging	40⅓	and	42¾	1,156
		Total for the three Companies	35 Exp.	averaging	40⅐	and	42⅓	2,903

* These trains are only admitted as express because of the tunnel into Glasgow, which is a mile long down a gradient of $\frac{1}{40}$, and is passed over very slowly. Otherwise the line between Glasgow and Edinburgh is one of the finest bits of nearly dead level in the country. Yet the local service is very slow; there are fourteen other trains labelled "express," whose average journey-speed amounts to only 33¾ (average time 1 hour 24 minutes). The Caledonian route, *viâ* Midcalder, is much harder.

Long Runs—

			Miles.		r.a.	
On the *G. & S. W.*	8	of	58½	run at	44⅓	All over 625 feet.
,, *N. British*	7	averaging	60⅓	,,	40⅓	All over 950 feet, and again over 850 for two trains.
,, *Caledonian*	8	,,	59½	,,	45½	All over 1,015 feet.
Total..	23	,,	59½	,,	43⅔	Over long hills of $\frac{1}{70}$ to $\frac{1}{150}$.

Longest—

$$G. \, \& \, S. \, W. \left\{ \begin{array}{l} \text{Dumfries and} \\ \text{Kilmarnock} \end{array} \right\} 58\tfrac{1}{2} \text{ in } 1 \; 18 = 45 \left\{ \begin{array}{l} 5.15 \text{ Newspaper} \\ \text{from St.Pancras} \end{array} \right.$$

Caledonian Carlisle to Carstairs $73\tfrac{1}{2}$ „ $1 \; 35^* = 48\tfrac{1}{2}$ Limited Mail.

$$N. \, British \left\{ \begin{array}{l} \text{Carlisle and} \\ \text{Edinburgh ..} \end{array} \right\} 98\tfrac{1}{4} \text{ „ } 2 \; 20 = 42 \quad \text{Night Express.}$$

Quickest—

Caledonian Carlisle to Beattock $39\tfrac{3}{4}$ in $- \; 48 = 49\tfrac{3}{8}$ 10.0 from Euston

$$N. \, British \left\{ \begin{array}{l} \text{Polmont to Cow-} \\ \text{lairs} \ldots \ldots \end{array} \right\} 23\tfrac{1}{2} \text{ „ } - \; 29 = 48\tfrac{5}{8} \left\{ \begin{array}{l} 10.0 \text{ from King's} \\ \text{Cross.} \end{array} \right.$$

$G. \, \& \, S. \, W.$ Carlisle to Dumfries 33 „ $- \; 42 = 47$ 3 down expresses

Best Expresses.—These have already been given in the comparison of the quickest running between England and Scotland by each of the three routes (see p. 93). We now show the total express service between London and Edinburgh and Glasgow.

Total Express Service between London and Scotland.

Miles	Route.	Number.	Average				Quickest is
			Time.	Journey-Speed.	Minutes Stopped.	Running-Average.	
	To and from Edinburgh		H. M.				
406	{ Midland and North British }	6	10 8	40	51	$43\tfrac{3}{4}$	9 hours 47 minutes = $41\tfrac{1}{2}$ journey-speed (8.0 down). [One other takes 11 hours 17 minutes = 36 (newspaper)]
$392\tfrac{1}{4}$	Great Northern, &c.	6 (2 up)	9 31	$41\tfrac{1}{4}$	50	$45\tfrac{1}{8}$	9 hours = $43\tfrac{3}{4}$ journey-speed (10.0 each way). [5 others (3 up) average 10 hours 17 minutes = 38]
$400\tfrac{1}{4}$	{ North Western and Caledonian }	4	9 55	$40\tfrac{1}{4}$	53	$44\tfrac{3}{8}$	9 hours 50 minutes = $40\tfrac{3}{4}$ journey-speed (10.0 down). [5 others (2 up) average 10 hours 48 minutes = 37]
		16 averaging		$40\tfrac{1}{4}$	and	$44\tfrac{5}{8}$	
	To and from Glasgow						
423	{ Midland and North British }	5 (3 up)	10 25	$40\tfrac{2}{3}$	51	$44\tfrac{1}{4}$	10 hours 20 minutes = 41 journey-speed (10.35 down). [2 others average 11 hours 28 minutes = 37]
$439\tfrac{3}{4}$	Great Northern, &c.	3 (1 up)	10 35	$41\tfrac{1}{4}$	59	$45\tfrac{4}{8}$	10 hours 20 minutes = $42\tfrac{1}{4}$ journey-speed (10.0 each way). [6 others average 11 hours 50 minutes = 37]
$401\tfrac{1}{2}$	{ North Western and Caledonian }	4	10 2¼	40	51	$43\tfrac{3}{4}$	10 hours = $40\tfrac{1}{4}$ journey-speed (10.0 each way)
		12 averaging		$40\tfrac{3}{4}$	and	$44\tfrac{1}{4}$	

* 4 minutes' stop.

Taking Express and Fast.

Between London and	Edinburgh.	Journey-Speed.	Glasgow.	Journey-Speed.
By E. Coast route there are	6 exp. + 5 fast	11 av. 39¾	3 exp. + 6 fast	9 av. 38¼
„ W. Coast „	4 „ +5 „	9 „ 38½	4 „ +5 „	9 „ 38⅛
„ Midland „	6 „ +1 „	7 „ 39¼	5 „ +2 „	7 „ 39¼
Total	—	27 av. 39¼	—	25 av. 38¾

Speed along gradients.—Before examining those sections of line over which our finest runs occur, we may notice the importance, if we would appreciate the speed of a train, of considering the severity and length of the gradients on which the running is done. We then see why it is impossible, on most of our routes, that the alliterative popular notion of "a mile a minute" on end can be carried out, and why the actual running-average of the best express subsides to a much more modest figure.

Taking the ordinary assumption that the resistance of the rails to the motion of a load along them is uniformly about 10 lbs. per ton, or $\frac{1}{224}$th of the load; then—

To maintain the same speed as on level ground, an engine ascending a gradient of* :

$$\frac{1}{224} \text{ must do twice as much work as it need on the level}$$
$$\frac{1}{112} \text{ „ 3 times „}$$
$$\frac{1}{75} \text{ „ 4 „ „}$$
$$\frac{1}{56} \text{ „ 5 „ „}$$
$$\frac{1}{45} \text{ „ 6 „ „}$$

(The engines of the Great Northern and Midland and other lines often exert 1,000 "horse-power" when ascending their gradients.)

But an engine made large enough to develope on occasion so great an excess over the work normally required of it on the level,

* $\frac{1}{100}$ is the most frequent gradient on the *Great Northern*; $\frac{1}{115}$, $\frac{1}{118}$, $\frac{1}{130}$ on the *Midland*, south of Leicester; $\frac{1}{112}$ to $\frac{1}{100}$ compose two-thirds of the *London, Chatham, and Dover* to Dover; $\frac{1}{130}$ to $\frac{1}{120}$ most of the *South Eastern* between New Cross and Tonbridge; $\frac{1}{112}$ is the *average* of the *Manchester, Sheffield, and Lincolnshire* between Sheffield and Manchester; $\frac{1}{130}$ on the *North Western*, south of Warrington, and $\frac{1}{75}$ to $\frac{1}{100}$ commonest north of Preston; $\frac{1}{100}$ in long pulls on the *Midland* between Settle and Carlisle; $\frac{1}{75}$ to $\frac{1}{115}$ plentiful on the *North British* between Carlisle and Edinburgh; $\frac{1}{80}$ to $\frac{1}{100}$ on the *Caledonian*, north of Lockerbie; $\frac{1}{100}$ to $\frac{1}{80}$ on the *Great Northern* between Wakefield and Bradford; $\frac{1}{45}$ on the *Great Western* west of Exeter; and 2 miles of $\frac{1}{37}$ on the *Midland* at Bromsgrove.

would be so heavy (leaving considerations of expense) that the permanent way would suffer from its momentum when descending. Therefore engines of the ordinary proportions, coming to a steep gradient, or to one which is not very steep but is very long (in which case the water supply shrinks), will not be able to keep on generating work enough to maintain their speed as fast as on the level. They must then submit to ascend at a speed which will not demand per second more work than the engine, coaxed to the limit of its extra-normal capacity, can supply. And if the gradient be very steep, the speed may be very low which will yet demand so much work as to reach this limit. ·

Now the *diminution* of speed thus produced throughout the *ascent* (and this itself, by deadening the draught, still further prevents the maintenance of pace) consumes many more minutes than could possibly be recovered, even by a *corresponding acceleration*, while descending the other side. For suppose that an engine able to draw its usual load 60 miles an hour on the level comes to an ascent of 10 miles of $\frac{1}{100}$, followed by a similar descent. Suppose speed falls to (an average of) 30 miles going up, and that going down the train runs (an average of) 90 miles an hour:—

Going *up* each mile occupies 2 minutes, therefore the 10-mile ascent takes 20 minutes.

Going *down* each mile occupies two-thirds of a minute, therefore the 10-mile descent takes $6\frac{3}{4}$ minutes. $26\frac{3}{4}$ minutes altogether up and down.

i.e., the whole 20 miles take $6\frac{3}{4}$ minutes more than they would have done on the level, a loss of $\frac{1}{3}$ *more* time. But now in actual practice the loss is greater again than this. For however slowly the gradient may cause the train to ascend, when it comes to descend the other side it must not as a rule be allowed to run faster than about 70 *miles an hour*. Curves, permanent way, wear and tear of carriages, and other considerations, forbid it.

And, therefore, as the favourable side of a gradient can never raise speed much above, while the unfavourable side may reduce it very much below, 60 miles an hour, we see why "a mile a minute" standard is too high for a country like England, and why the net effect of gradients is mostly dead loss uncompensated, especially for expresses whose ordinary speed on the level comes near to 60 miles an hour.

It is true that were rails frictionless, and stopping stations on the tops of watersheds, the extra momentum gained going down-hill might help in the next *ascent* so that the average pace need not be much less than over an equal distance on the level. But in practice, first, there is friction, which soon nips off the superadded speed; and, secondly, most of our important towns are on rivers or otherwise near sea level, placed as it were on either side of a roof near the bottom. Thus the train tackles the ascent in the most unfavourable circumstances, and has to stop again when the conditions are most in its favour.

Those lines then whose routes are comparatively level should exhibit better running-averages than the others, especially if trains are heavy. And when we see the "running-average" of *Midland* trains over Derbyshire and Westmoreland heights (long pulls up $\frac{1}{90}$ and $\frac{1}{100}$), of the *Caledonian* or *North British* over Lowland watersheds ($\frac{1}{80}$ and $\frac{1}{70}$), or of *Manchester, Sheffield, & Lincolnshire* up and down the Pennine ($\frac{1}{125}$), we must admire, not so much the dashing descent, as the persistent strength with which those engines mount.

We will now describe the gradients of those portions of the three great lines and their Scotch connections which we have not yet given, viz., the hilly sections, and notice the best runs made over these sections (the G.N.R. is scarcely a hilly section).

The runs are these :—*

Between	Miles.	Time Taken.	Running Average.	Done by
		H. M.		
A. Grantham and King's Cross (G.N.R.)	105½	2 4	51	2 up fast exp. from Manch.
B. St. Pancras and Leicester (Midland)....	99¼	2 7	47	Down Scotch express
C. Carlisle and Edinburgh (N. British)....	98¼	2 20	42	Night exp.—in summer
D. Derby and Liverpool (Midland)	91½	2 4	44¼	12.0 from St. Pancras
E. Skipton and Carlisle („)	86¾	1 55	45⅓	Night express—summer
F. Carlisle and Carstairs (Caledonian)	73½	1 35	48½	Lim. mail {It stops 4′ at summit
G. Carlisle and Carnforth (N. Western) ..	62¾	1 25	44¼	Limited mail
b. Bedford and Kentish Town (Midland)	48	1 –	48	All the Manch. expresses

A. From King's Cross the line rises 1½ miles at $\frac{1}{110}$ to *Holloway*, runs 3 nearly level to *Hornsey*, then rises 8 miles of $\frac{1}{200}$ to *Potter's Bar*, about 350 feet above sea; falls 4 miles gently and 2 at $\frac{1}{200}$ to a little past *Hatfield;* rises 5, 3½ of which are $\frac{1}{200}$, to *Knebworth*, 360 feet; falls gently 4 miles to *Stevenage*, and then down 7 miles of $\frac{1}{200}$ to *Arlesey* (35½ miles from London). From here it runs 24 miles nearly level (with the Ouse) to *Huntingdon;* then rises 3 miles $\frac{1}{200}$ before *Abbot's Ripton*, and falls again 5 miles $\frac{1}{200}$ on to the Fens (67 miles from London). Then follow 24 miles nearly level to 2 miles beyond *Essendine;* and from this it rises 9 miles

* *The Longest Run outside England is in France.*

Laroche to Dijon (P., L., and Med.)	99	2 41	37	{7.15 p.m. from Paris. 1st cl. only

(1 mile rest) of $\frac{1}{300}$ and $\frac{1}{176}$ to *Stoke* tunnel (lias-oolite), 370 feet above sea; then falls 5 miles of $\frac{1}{200}$ to *Grantham*, 105½ miles.

[Thus the long run of the up Manchester express is over a course by no means quite easy, having two adverse spells of $\frac{1}{300}$ for 5 and 7 miles respectively. The slack through Peterborough and after Finsbury Park must also be considered. The corresponding *down* trains take two minutes longer, as the adverse spells are then 8 and 8 (with a rest) of $\frac{1}{300}$.]

The rest of the course from *Grantham* to *Doncaster* is nearly level, dropping down gently to *Newark* (120 miles), with a short rise and fall (3 miles $\frac{1}{200}$) on each side of the *Askham* tunnel near Retford.

Between *Doncaster* and *Leeds* there are two steep bits, a 7-mile rise and 4-mile fall (chiefly $\frac{1}{150}$) before *Wakefield*, and a 5-mile rise after to the *Ardsley* summit (385 feet), from which the line falls 4 miles $\frac{1}{100}$ to *Leeds* (185¾ miles). From Ardsley the Bradford trains continue with a steep rise for 8 miles ($\frac{1}{70}$ to $\frac{1}{132}$) to about 750 feet, then drop very steeply 4 miles (2 of $\frac{1}{50}$ to $\frac{1}{40}$) into *Bradford* (192½ miles). Thus the speed to Bradford is very good. In 1880 it was better, as four trains ran between Bradford and London in four hours. [And on 24th June, 1882, H.R.H. the Prince of Wales came from Bradford to London in 3 hours 48 minutes, including a stop of 5 minutes at Grantham. This was a journey-speed of 50½, and a running-average of 52. This is perhaps better than the more level trip made by the Lord Mayor and suite on 31st July, 1880, when the run to York from King's Cross was done in 3 hours 37 minutes, including 10 minutes' stop at Grantham, a journey-speed of 52, and running-average of 54¾.]

B. *St. Pancras to Leicester :—*

From St. Pancras the line rises (with 1½ mile rest) 12½ miles moderately steep (5 of $\frac{1}{176}$) to *Elstree*; falls 2½ of $\frac{1}{200}$, rises 5 miles (past *St. Albans*) of $\frac{1}{176}$, then runs about level for 11 miles (past *Luton*) to 430 feet above sea (34 miles from London); from which it falls 16 miles, 11 of which are $\frac{1}{200}$, into *Bedford*. From Bedford it rises gently 6 miles and 4 miles steep ($\frac{1}{120}$) to *Sharnbrook* summit; drops 3 miles of $\frac{1}{120}$ and 1 of $\frac{1}{200}$ to *Wellingborough*; rises gently for 7 miles to *Kettering*; then rises steeply 6¼ miles, $\frac{1}{132}$ or $\frac{1}{165}$, to *Desborough* summit, 490 feet; drops again 4 miles of $\frac{1}{132}$ to *Market Harborough*; rises 5 miles gently and 2 of $\frac{1}{132}$ to *Kibworth* summit (420 feet); and falls 9 miles gradually into *Leicester*, 99¾ miles.

This, though the elevations are not very great, is a very trying long run, the second half being much harder than the first. The running average of 47 attained over these steep ups and downs by the Scotch express with its heavy train is a first rate performance.

b. So too are the every day runs of the Liverpool and Manchester

H

expresses, which regularly stop at Kentish Town platform one hour after leaving Bedford, 48 miles, with a long pull of 11 miles $\frac{1}{100}$ up (2 miles rest). The 5.15 a.m. newspaper train runs easily in the hour from *St. Pancras* to Bedford, $49\frac{3}{4}$ miles, and then does the $49\frac{1}{4}$ miles to Leicester in the next hour. These are the sort of things that do not happen out of England.

C. *Carlisle to Edinburgh*, by "Waverley" route :—

The North British on leaving Carlisle fluctuates for 11 miles with moderate steepness without rising, then rises 8 miles, 4 of which are $\frac{1}{100}$, and falls again 2 miles to *Kershope Foot*, from which it rises 4 miles moderately ($\frac{1}{200}$ to $\frac{1}{800}$) to a mile past *Newcastleton*, 315 feet. Here it mounts up very steeply $9\frac{1}{2}$ miles, 8 of which are $\frac{1}{75}$, to the summit a mile and a half beyond *Ricarton Junction* (955 feet, 34 miles from Carlisle). From this it drops 11 miles, mostly $\frac{1}{75}$ to $\frac{1}{100}$, down to *Hawick* on the Teviot, along the left bank of which it rises 6 miles, and falls 6 rather steeply ($\frac{1}{110}$ to $\frac{1}{100}$) to *St. Boswell's*, then fluctuates easily for $6\frac{1}{2}$ miles to *Galashiels* on the Tweed (315 feet, $64\frac{1}{2}$ miles from Carlisle). Here it runs up beside the *Gala Water* rather steeply for 16 miles (mostly $\frac{1}{110}$ and $\frac{1}{120}$) to the summit near *Falahill* (850 feet, 80 miles from Carlisle), from which it drops 15 miles, 8 of which are $\frac{1}{70}$, to *Portobello Junction*, rises a mile and a half easy, and mounts $1\frac{1}{4}$ of $\frac{1}{78}$ into Edinburgh, $98\frac{1}{4}$ miles.

This is undoubtedly the hardest of all the routes in the kingdom over which any train makes a Long Run at express speed. Twice to climb such gradients and yet keep on for 98 miles without a halt, is a feat of Homeric nature, and a testimonial to English engineers.

D. *Derby to Liverpool, viâ* Stockport :—

The Midland runs beside the Derwent for about 20 miles from Derby, rising gently (steepest $\frac{1}{330}$) to *Ambergate*, 9 miles, and a little more to *Rowsley*. Here it leaves the Derwent, and winds up for 12 miles in a series of curves along the valley of the Wye, ascending more steeply as it proceeds. Soon after *Miller's Dale* ($31\frac{1}{2}$ miles) it leaves the Wye and mounts up 6 miles about $\frac{1}{90}$ to the *Peak Forest* tunnel, 999 feet above sea ($37\frac{1}{2}$ miles) from which it drops 10 miles very steeply (about $\frac{1}{90}$) to *Marple*, $48\frac{3}{4}$ miles. From Marple it falls again steeply to *Stockport* ($53\frac{3}{4}$ miles). From Stockport to *Warrington* is $19\frac{3}{4}$ miles nearly level, and from Warrington 18 miles of short fluctuations ($\frac{1}{330}$) or level bring it to *Liverpool*, $91\frac{1}{2}$ miles—a fine Long Run done well within its time.

This run (which is contingent on signals at Stockport and Warrington) is coincident with an improvement lately made in the Liverpool trains of the North Western, which now runs three (two down) in $4\frac{1}{2}$ hours. The Midland now send their Liverpool carriages on *viâ* Stockport instead of Manchester, and some are run as distinct trains from Derby. The quickest Midland train runs from Liverpool in 5 hours 5 minutes; 27 miles and 35 minutes longer than the North Western, but a much finer performance.

E. *Skipton* to *Carlisle.* (Midland):—

The line rises 8 miles of $\frac{1}{110}$, and falls 5 averaging $\frac{1}{200}$ to 2 miles south of *Settle*, about 390 feet above sea. From here it mounts up 15 miles of $\frac{1}{100}$ to *Blea Moor* tunnel, 1,130 feet ($1\frac{1}{2}$ miles long). It then undulates nearly level for 10 miles (over five viaducts and through three tunnels) to *Ais Gill* sidings, 1,170 feet above sea. From this it drops 15 miles, 11 of which are $\frac{1}{100}$, to *Ormside*, and runs 3 miles nearly level to *Appleby*, 540 feet; then falls 2 miles $\frac{1}{120}$ and 13 gently to *Lazonby;* undulates 7 miles about same height, and falls 7 miles of $\frac{1}{132}$ (1 mile level) into *Carlisle*, $86\frac{3}{4}$ miles, about 70 feet above sea.

There are two things equally fine about this run, the view from the top of the watershed, and the style in which the express engine ascends. The day express, the heaviest, reaches the tunnel 22 minutes after passing Settle, $13\frac{1}{4}$ miles, an *average* speed of $37\frac{1}{2}$ miles per hour. It therefore makes each second a vertical step of $6\frac{1}{2}$ inches and a forward movement of 55 feet.

F. *Carlisle* and *Carstairs.* (Caledonian):—

The line falls gently $7\frac{1}{2}$ miles to nearly sea level, rises 7 about $\frac{1}{200}$, falls 4 gently, rises 4 of about $\frac{1}{200}$ past *Ecclefechan*, falls 7 gently (past *Lockerbie*), and rises 7 gently to the thirty-sixth mile from Carlisle. It then rises 4 miles of $\frac{1}{200}$, and mounts up steeply $9\frac{1}{2}$ of about $\frac{1}{80}$ to the summit, 1,015 feet above sea, from which it falls moderately fluctuating for 22 miles to Carstairs, 640 feet, $73\frac{1}{2}$ miles. The ascent is made beside *Evan Water*, a branch of the Annan, and the descent follows the Clyde. [To Glasgow the line continues with the Clyde in a steep descent (chiefly $\frac{1}{100}$), while to Edinburgh it turns east, rises again to 870 feet, and falls steeply ($\frac{1}{100}$) to the capital.]

The runs of several expresses over this watershed are extremely creditable, particularly that of the down mail, which, as shown in the table, *averages* a speed of $48\frac{1}{2}$ on the $73\frac{1}{2}$ miles between Carlisle and Carstairs. The last 10 miles before the summit can hardly take less than 23 minutes ($\frac{1}{80}$), and this leaves only 68 minutes for the remaining $63\frac{1}{2}$ miles, an average speed of 56 miles an hour, which is good driving.

G. *Carlisle* to *Carnforth*:—

Starting from about 70 feet above sea, the North Western rises 4 miles averaging $\frac{1}{133}$ and 7 averaging $\frac{1}{200}$, then runs nearly level (past *Penrith*) for 9 miles; here it mounts up 10 miles averaging $\frac{1}{145}$, to *Shap* summit, 915 feet above sea ($30\frac{1}{2}$ miles from Carlisle).

From this it drops very steeply (and sharp curves) 4 miles of $\frac{1}{78}$ and 2 of $\frac{1}{147}$ to *Tebay*, from which it rises again a little 5 miles to *Grayrigg*, 600 feet; from here it drops 13 miles averaging $\frac{1}{130}$ and $2\frac{1}{2}$ of $\frac{1}{117}$ to *Carnforth*, only a few feet above sea level. [From Carnforth to Euston (except a mile at Lancaster and a little between Preston and Wigan) the track is very easy, the worst gradients (except 3 miles $\frac{1}{177}$ into Crewe from the south) being $\frac{1}{330}$].

This North Western route is easier than the Midland for *down* trains, but rather harder for the *up;* as though the gradients in the latter case are not quite so steep, yet the North Western climbs 850 feet from Carlisle to Shap in 31 miles, as against 1,100 feet from Carlisle to Ais Gill in 46 miles. The curves are also sharper than in the case of the Midland, which was built regardless of expense. But allowing for this, the speed of the Midland remains a better performance.

On any of the seven hill sections above described, a man who wishes to experience "70 miles an hour" can be satisfied every day. At two points in particular, when he drops like a star from Peak Forest into the smoke of Manchester, or when the lonely "Maiden Paps" disappear behind him as he swoops down the curves of Slitrig Water into Hawick, he will not feel easy till he learns that good continuous brakes are waiting charged beneath his feet.

We can now sum up the results for the whole kingdom :—

I.—NUMBER AND MILEAGE OF EXPRESSES RUN BY EACH COMPANY.

Extent of System in Miles.		Distinct Expresses.	Average Journey-Speed.	Running-Average.	Express Mileage.
1,773	North Western	$\left\{\begin{matrix}54\\28\end{matrix}\right\}82$	40¾	43$\frac{1}{10}$	10,400
1,260	Midland	66	41¼	45	8,860
635	Great Northern	$\left\{\begin{matrix}48\\19\end{matrix}\right\}67$	43	46¼	6,780
907	Great Eastern	34	41	43¼	3,040
2,267	Great Western	18	42	46¼	2,600
290	Manch.,Sheff., and Linc.	49	43	44⅜	2,318
1,519	North Eastern	19	40½	43¼	2,110
435¼	Brighton	15	41¼	42	1.270*
767	Caledonian	16	40½	42¼	1,155
382	South Eastern...............	12	41	41¼	940
329	Glasgow and S.Western	8	41¾	43¼	920
796¼	London and S. Western	3	41¼	44⅜	890†
984	North British	11	39	41	830
153	Chatham and Dover	9	42	43¼	690
		409	41¾	44⅜	42,795

* The running-average of *expresses* is 42, but is 41¾ for the 1,270 mileage, which includes Long runs of some fast trains.

† The running-average of the *expresses* is 44½, but is 44 for the 890 mileage, which includes Long runs of some fast trains.

A total of four hundred and nine express trains, whose average journey-speed is $41\frac{3}{5}$, and which run 42,795 miles at an average "running-average" of $44\frac{1}{3}$ miles per hour.

If we arrange the Companies according to their *speed* instead of their mileage, the order is:—

II.—EXPRESS MILEAGE ARRANGED ACCORDING TO SPEED.

	Average r.a.	Miles.		Average r.a.	Miles.
Great Northern	$46\frac{1}{2}$	6,780	Great Eastern	$43\frac{1}{4}$	3,040
Great Western	$46\frac{1}{4}$	2,600*	North Eastern	$43\frac{1}{4}$	2,110
Midland	45	8,860	Chatham and Dover	$43\frac{1}{8}$	690
Man., Shef., and Lin.	$44\frac{5}{8}$	2,318	Caledonian	$42\frac{3}{4}$	1,155
Lond. and S. Western	44	890	Brighton	$41\frac{3}{4}$	1,270
North Western	$43\frac{7}{10}$	10,400	South Eastern	$41\frac{3}{4}$	940
Glas. and S. Western	$43\frac{1}{2}$	920	North British	41	825

* Not reckoning mileage west of *Exeter*.

Express Routes arranged in Order of Difficulty of Gradients, &c.

North British	Chatham and Dover	Brighton
Caledonian	South Eastern	North Western
Man., Sheff., and Lin.	Great Northern	North Eastern
Midland	South Western	Great Western
Glas. and S. Western	Great Eastern	

Note.—This order is only approximate, reckoning besides *gradients* such adverse conditions as the number of enforced *slackenings* past junctions, &c., or the time lost in London *suburbs*, &c.

III.—LONG RUNS IN ENGLAND.

See p. 92

On the Midland................	104,	averaging	53	m. at an av. r.a. of	$46\frac{1}{2}$	(5,512 m.)
„ North Western ...	98,	„	60	„ „	45	(5,880 „)
„ Great Northern....	49,	„	$73\frac{3}{4}$	„ „	50	(3,616 „)
„ Great Western	24,	„	56	„ „	$48\frac{1}{2}$	(1,344 „)
„ Great Eastern	24,	„	$56\frac{3}{4}$	„ „	$42\frac{1}{2}$	(1,362 „)
„ Brighton	25,	„	46	„ „	42	(1,150 „)
„ North Eastern	20,	„	56	„ „	$44\frac{5}{8}$	(1,120 „)
„ South Western....	13,	„	$47\frac{1}{2}$	„ „	$44\frac{3}{8}$	(615 „)
„ South Eastern	12,	„	$66\frac{1}{4}$	„ „	$42\frac{1}{3}$	(795 „)
„ Chatham & Dover	8,	„	63	„ „	45	(504 „)
„ Caledonian	8,	„	$59\frac{1}{2}$	„ „	$45\frac{1}{2}$	(476 „)
„ Glasgow and S. Western	8,	„	$58\frac{1}{2}$	„ „	$44\frac{1}{2}$	(468 „)
„ Man., Shef. & L.	8,	„	$48\frac{3}{4}$	„ „	$43\frac{1}{2}$	(390 „)
„ North British	7,	„	$60\frac{1}{2}$	„ „	$40\frac{1}{2}$	(423 „)
Total	408,	averaging	58	miles at a r.a. of	$45\frac{3}{4}$	(23,650 m.)

Note.—From this it will be seen that the three great companies run 61 per cent. of the whole *express mileage*, and 63 per cent. of the whole number of *long runs*.

Long Runs arranged According to Speed.

This would be very similar to the order in Table II, except that the long runs of the Manchester, Sheffield, and Lincoln occur on its steepest section, and hence this line would come near the bottom.

IV.—FASTEST RUNS IN ENGLAND.

On the	Between	Distance.	Time.	Running-Average.	Done by
		Miles.	H. M.		
Man. Sheff. and Linc.	Manchester & Warrington	16	– 18	= 53⅓	16 trains daily
Great Western	Paddington and Swindon	77½	1 27	= 53⅓	4 Exeter expresses
Great Northern	Hitchin & Peterboro'	44⅔	– 50	= 53	5.0 P.M. Sundays
„	Grantham and Doncaster	50½	– 58	= 52¼	1.15 from King's Cross
„	„ London	105½	2 4	= 51	2 Manchester exp. up
North Western	Northampton & Willesden	60½	1 10	= 51⅓	9.30 from Birmingham
„	Rugby „	77¼	1 32	= 50½	7.30 „
Midland	Liverpool and Stockport	37¾	– 45	= 50½	{ With or without stop; 4 trains
„	St. Pancras and Kettering	72¼	1 27	= 49¼	10.0 from London
„	Bedford and Kentish Town	48	1 –	= 48	All Manch. expresses
North Eastern	York and Darlington	44¼	– 53	= 50	3.25 from York
Caledonian	Carlisle and Beattock	39¾	– 48	= 49⅔	10.0 from Euston
„	„ Carstairs	73¼	1 31	= 48½	8.50 „
Great Eastern	Lincoln and Spalding	38¼	– 47	= 48⅔	3 or 4 trains
North British	{ Polmont and Cowlairs (between Edinburgh and Glasgow)............	23⅓	– 29	= 48⅔	10.0 from King's Cross
Glas. and S.Western	Carlisle and Dumfries	33	– 42	= 47	10.35 from St. Pancras
Brighton	London Bridge & Brighton	50½	1 5	= 46½	5.0 down
Chatham and Dover	Herne Hill and Dover........	74	1 36	= 46½	7.40 A.M. from Victoria
South Western	{ Yeovil Junction and Exeter (ticket) .... }	48⅓	1 3	= 46⅓	3 down trains
„ *Eastern*	Cannon Street and Dover	74¼	1 39	= 45	7.40 A.M. from Cannon St.

V.—FASTEST RUNS OVER STEEP GROUND (*arranged in Order of Severity of Route*).

Between	Distance.	Time.	Running-Average.	Company.
	Miles.	H. M.		
Carlisle and Edinburgh	98¼	2 20	= 42	North British
„ Carstairs	73¼	1 31	= 48⅓	Caledonian
„ Carnforth	62¾	1 25	= 44¼	North Western
„ Skipton	86¾	1 55	= 45¼	Midland
Derby and Liverpool	91¼	2 4	= 44¼	„
St. Pancras and Leicester	99¼	2 7	= 47	„

Mileage of Long Runs over Steep Ground.

	Runs.	Averaging	Running-Average.	Mileage.
In the Scotch *Lowlands,* by the three Cos.	23	59¼ miles	43¾	1,368
„ *Derbyshire & Westmoreland,* by Mid.	16	66 „	44	1,056
„ *Lake District,* by North Western........	12	60¾ „	43	729
Across the *Pennine,* by M.S. & L.	4	41 „	40½	164
Total hill runs	55	60½ miles	43½	3,317

Note.—This table does perhaps more credit to English railways than either of the others.

VI.—LONGEST RUNS IN ENGLAND.

	Miles.	Company.	Run in	Running-Average.
			H. M.	
1. Grantham and King's Cross	105¼	Great Northern	2 4	— 51
2. Leicester and St. Pancras	99¼	Midland	2 7	— 47
3. Carlisle and Edinburgh........	98¼	North British	2 20	— 42
4. Nuneaton and Willesden	91½	Lond. & N. Wstn.	1 57	— 47
5. Derby and Liverpool............	91½	Midland	2 4	— 44¼
6. Preston and Carlisle	90	Lond. & N. Wstn.	2 10	— 41¼
7. Skipton „	86¾	Midland	1 55	— 45¼
8. Chester and Holyhead	84¼	Lond. & N. Wstn.	2 –	— 42¼
9. Rugby and Euston...............	82¾	„	1 50	— 45
10. Grantham and York	82¼	Great Northern	1 39	— 50
11. Newcastle „	80¼	North Eastern	1 42	— 47¼
12. Victoria and Dover	78	L. C. and Dover	1 45	— 44¾
13. Paddington and Swindon	77½	Great Western	1 27	— 53½
14. Cannon Street and Dover	74¼	South Eastern	1 39	— 45
15. Carlisle and Carstairs............	73¼	Caledonian	1 31	— 48¼

VII.—TOWNS BEST SUPPLIED WITH EXPRESSES TO AND FROM LONDON.

Distance.	Between		In Summer.		
Miles.					
82¾, 84¾	*Rugby*	and London there are	50	express journeys daily	
182½—203	*Manchester*	„	42	„	
105½	*Grantham*	„	37	„	(19 up)
177—200	*Stockport*	„	35	„	(17 „)
124—127¾	*Nottingham*	„	35	„	(17 „)
158, 160	*Crewe*	„	34	„	(16 „)
158—164	*Sheffield*	„	33	„	(17 „)
76¼	*Peterborough*	„	29	„	(16 „)
185½—204	*Leeds*	„	28	„	
193½—237½	*Liverpool*	„	27	„	(14 „)
156	*Doncaster*	„	27	„	(12 „)
182¼—219½	*Warrington*	„	27	„	(13 „)
55½—58	*Cambridge*	„	24	„	
138½	*Retford*	„	23	„	(11 up)
192½—193½	*Bradford*	„	22	„	
128¾, 138½	*Derby*	„	21	„	(10 up)
65¾	*Northampton*	„	21	„	(9 „)
188	*York*	„	20	„	(9 „)
99¼	*Leicester*	„	20	„	
49¾	*Bedford*	„	17	„	(9 „)
392½—406	*Edinburgh*	„	16	„	(7 „)
299¼—310	*Carlisle*	„	14	„	
77	*Swindon*	„	13	„	(6 „)
51¾	*Colchester*	„	13	„	(5 „)
47¾	*Basingstoke*	„	13	„	(6 „)
401½—439¾	*Glasgow*	„	12	„	
113—129	*Birmingham*	„	12	„	
130¼—143½	*Lincoln*	„	12	„	
232	*Darlington*	„	11	„	
179—213	*Chester*	„	11	„	
268¼	*Newcastle*	„	10	„	
118½	*Bristol*	„	10	„	

N.B.—The express service to and from *London* is generally identical with the *entire* express service between towns; the only separate *local* expresses are between Manchester and Liverpool; between Bristol, Birmingham, Derby, York, Leeds, and Hull; between Newcastle and York; and Leeds and York.

VIII.—IMPORTANT TOWNS BADLY OFF FOR EXPRESS COMMUNICATION.

	No. of Lond. Expresses.	Population.	
Portsmouth...........	*none*	127,000	Chief dockyard in kingdom, &c.
Southampton	„	60,000	
Swansea	„	65,000	Most rapidly growing ports in England
Cardiff	1	85,000	
Yarmouth	*none*	46,000	
Norwich	1	87,000	
Milford Haven	*none*	—	Port for Ireland and possibly America
Falmouth	„	—	Last port westward
Hull	3	—	Fourth port in kingdom
Weymouth	*none*	14,000	Port for G. Western route to France
Sunderland	1	120,000	Port, shipbuilding centre, &c.
Middlesborough	3	60,000	120 blast furnaces, &c.

IX.—QUICKEST TIME BETWEEN IMPORTANT TOWNS AND LONDON
during the Summer of 1883.

Miles.		Up or Down	Time. H.	M.	Journey-Speed.	Minutes Stopped.	Running-Average.	Number of Stoppages.	Company.
540¼	Aberdeen	d.	14	50	36¾	114	*not exp.*	16	N. Western and Caln.
277¼	Appleby	,,	6	46	41	40	45½	4	Midland
47¾	Basingstoke	,,	1	3	45¼	—	45¼	—	Lon. and S. Western
106¾	Bath	,,	2	13	48	10	52	1	Great Western
49¾	Bedford	,,	1	-	49¾	—	49¾	—	Midland
335	Berwick	,,	7	38	43¾	42	48¼	3	G.N. and N.E.
228½	Birkenhead	,,	5	8	44½	16	47	5	Great Western
113	Birmingham	up	2	35	43¾	9	46½	4	Lon. and N. Western
129¼	,,	d.	2	42	47¼	4	49	1	Great Western
115¾	Bournemouth	,,	3	9	36¾	15	*not exp.*	6	Lon. and S. Western
193	Bradford	up	4	15	45¾	17	48¾	6	Great Northern
209¼	,,		4	55	42¾	23	46	5	Midland
50½	Brighton	d.	1	5	46¾	—	46¾	—	L.B. and S.C.
118¼	Bristol	both	2	36	45¼	13	49¾	2	Great Western
163	Buxton	up	4	5	40	28	44½	6	Midland
55½	Cambridge	d.	1	15	44¾	—	44¾	—	Great Eastern
58	,,	up	1	15*	46½	3	48½	2	,, Northern
68	Canterbury	,,	1	38	41¼	2	42½	1	South Eastern
61¾	,,	d.	1	23	44¾	2	45¾	1	Lon.Chat. and Dover
170½	Cardiff	,,	4	21	39½	25	43½	5	{ Great Western (the only express)
299¼	Carlisle	up	7	15	41¼	41	45¼	5	Lon. and N. Western
307¾	,,	d.	7	20	42	31	45½	7	Midland
34	Chatham	both	-	50	40¾	2	42¼	1	Lon.Chat. and Dover
122½	Cheltenham	d.	3	15	37¾	24	*not exp.*	4	Great Western
179	Chester	up	4	10	43	21	47	3	Lon. and N. Western
213	,,	d.	4	50	44	15	46½	5	Great Western
152½	Chesterfield	,,	3	18	46	10	48½	2	Midland
51¾	Colchester	,,	1	10	44½	—	44¾	—	Great Eastern
94	Coventry	up	2	4	45½	6	47½	2	Lon. and N. Western
158	Crewe	,,	3	30	45	11	47½	2	,,
232¼	Darlington	,,	5	19	43¾	36	49¼	2	Great Northern
128¾	Derby	both	2	53	44¾	14	48¼	3	Midland
156	Doncaster	d.	3	13	48½	7	50½	2	Great Northern
74¼	Dover	,,	1	39	45	—	45	—	South Eastern
78	,,	up	1	45	44½	—	44¾	—	Lon.Chat. and Dover
330	Dublin	d.	11	30	28½ in·luding la nd and sea			8	Lon. and N. Western
471¼	Dundee	,,	12	10	38½	70	*not exp.*	14	,,
254	Durham	up	5	59	42½	42	48	8	G.N. and N.E.
65½	Eastbourne	,,	1	27	45	0	45	0	L.B. & S.C.
392½	Edinburgh	both	9	-	43¾	49	48	4—5	East Coast Route
400¼	,,	d.	9	50	40¾	51	44¾	8	West ,, ,,
406	,,	,,	9	47	41¼	55	44¼	9	Midland ,, ,,
70½	Ely	,,	1	38	43	2	44	1	Great Eastern
171¼	Exeter	,,	4	3	42½	15	45	5	Lon. and S. Western
194	,,	,,	4	14	45¾	23	50½	4	Great Western

* 12.0 up express. This train has to slacken at *Shelford Junction*, and makes two stops, on ascending gradients, one at *Royston*, the other *Hitchin.*

IX *Contd.*—QUICKEST TIME BETWEEN IMPORTANT TOWNS AND LONDON *during the Summer of* 1883.

Miles.		Up or Down.	Time. H.	Time. M.	Journey-Speed.	Minutes Stopped.	Running-Average.	Number of Stoppages.	Company.
312½	Falmouth	up	8	30	36¾	52	*not exp.*	16	Great Western
69	Folkestone............	both	1	45	39⅓	—	39⅓	—	South Eastern
401½	Glasgow	both	10	-	40⅙	51	44	8	West Coast
423	„	d.	10	20	41	56	45	8	Midland
439¾	„	both	10	20	42½	59	47	9	East Coast
105½	Grantham	up	2	4	51	—	51	—	Great Northern
114	Gloucester	d.	2	53	39⅓	14	43	3	„ Western
199½	Halifax	„	4	45	42	25	46	10	„ Northern
69¼	Harwich................	„	1	46	39⅓	—	39⅓	—	„ Eastern
60⅓	Hastings	up	1	37	37⅔	3	*not exp.*	2	South Eastern
263¾	Holyhead	d.	6	35	40	31	43½	7	L. and N.W.
188⅓	Huddersfield........	both	4	35	41	33	46¾	6	G.N. and M.S. & L.
197	Hull	d.	4	50	40¾	32	45⅝	8	G.N. and N.E.
226	Ilfracombe	„	6	20	35¾	40	*not exp.*	14	South Western
594½	Inverness	„	16	40	35⅝	120	*not exp.*	25	N.W & Highland
68¾	Ipswich	both	1	40	41¼	—	41⅓	14	Great Eastern
230¼	Lancaster	d.	5	40	40⅝	39	46	4	L. and N.W.
106	Leamington	„	2	13	47¾	4	49¼	1	Great Western
185½	Leeds	up	4	-	46⅓	12	48⅛	5	„ Northern
196	„	both	4	30	43½	14	46	3	Midland, *viâ* Trent
204	„	d.	4	30	45⅓	16	48	3	„ *viâ* Melton
99½	Leicester	„	2	7	47	—	47	—	Midland
130½	Lincoln	„	3	5	42¼	23	48½	4	Great Northern
143½	„	„	3	23	42⅔	9	44⅛	—	„ Eastern
193½	Liverpool	„	4	30	43	20	46⅔	5	L. and N.W.
220¼	„	up	5	5	43⅓	24	47	7	Midland
229	„	d.	5	25	see *Bir*	*kenhead*	for railwa	y portion	Great Western
237½	„	„	5	55	40	33	44½	10	G.N. and M.S. & L.
170	Macclesfield	„	4	5	41⅝	16	44½	5	North Western
189	Manchester	both	4	30	42	24	46	6	„
191¼	„	up	4	35	41¾	21	45⅛	6	Midland
203	„	both	4	30	45	10	47	—	G.N. and M.S. & L.
73¾	Margate	both	1	45	42	4	43⅘	2	Chatham and Dover
238½	Middlesborough	d.	5	44	41⅝	24	44¾	7	G.N. and N.E.
285½	Milford Haven	up	8	-	35⅝	62	*not exp.*	12	Great Western
120	Newark	d.	2	36	46	7	48⅓	3	„ Northern
268¼	Newcastle	„	6	7	44	37	48¾	2	G.N. and N.E.
158½	Newport (Mon.)	„	4	-	39⅝	22	43⅜	4	Great Western
65¾	Northampton	„	1	22	48	—	48	—	Lon. and N.Western
124	Norwich	„	3	10	39	14	42¼	3	Great Eastern
127¾	Nottingham	„	2	48	45⅜	7	47⅜	4	„ Northern
124	„	„	2	35	48	4	49¼	1	Midland
63¼	Oxford	„	1	18	49	—	49	—	Great Western
326½	Penzance	up	8	55	36½	55	*not exp.*	18	„
450½	Perth	d.	11	25	39½	56	43	13	N.Western and Caln.
462	„	up	11	30	40	75	45	14	East Coast Route
477½	„	d.	12	23	38½	72	42¾	13	Midland
76¼	Peterborough	„	1	30	50⅛	—	50⅛	—	Great Northern
246½	Plymouth	„	6	-	41	35	45½	9	„ Western
73½	Portsmouth	up	1	55	38⅓	8	*not exp.*	4	Lon. and S. Western
209¼	Preston	„	4	50	43¼	19	46⅓	3	Lon. and N.Western
49½	Queenborough	d.	1	25	35	6	*not exp.*	2	Lon.Chat. and Dover

IX *Contd.*—QUICKEST TIME BETWEEN IMPORTANT TOWNS AND LONDON
during the Summer of 1883.

Miles.		Up or Down.	Time. H. M.	Journey-Speed.	Minutes Stopped.	Running-Average.	Number of Stoppages.	Company.
79	Ramsgate	both	2 —	39½	8	42¾	4	Lon.Chat.and Dover
83¾	„ from Londn. Bridge	up	2 6	40	6	42	3	South Eastern
35¾	Reading	d.	— 46	46¾	—	46¾	—	Great Western
138¼	Retford	up	2 54	47¼	6	49¾	2	„ Northern
82¾	Rugby	„	1 45	47¼	2	48	1	Lon. and N.Western
83½	Salisbury	d.	1 56	43	5	45	2	Lon. and S. Western
230¾	Scarborough	„	5 35	41½	42	47¼	5	G.N. and N.E.
164¼	Sheffield................	„	3 35	46	11	48½	2	Midland
162	„	„	3 23	48	5	49	1	Great Northern
163	Shrewsbury ;........	„	3 48	43	18	46¾	4	Lon. and N.Western
171	„	„	3 47	45¼	10	47¾	3	Great Western
223	Skipton	„	5 22	41¼	29	45¾	6	Mid. (*viâ* Sheffield)
264	Snowdon*	„	8 50	30	80	35	20	Lon. and N.Western
79	Southampton	„	2 4	38½	10	*not exp.*	4	Lon. and S.Western
133½	Stafford	„	3 —	44½	8	46½	2	„
184	Stockport	„	4 19˙	42¾	20	46	6	Lon. and N.Western
182¼	„	up	4 18	42½	18	45¾	5	Midland
199¾	„	d.	4 59	40	29	44¾	7	G.N. and M.S. & L.
666	Strome Ferry	„	20 50	32	180	37½	37	L.and N.W., Caln., and Highland
216	Swansea................	„	6 —	36	40	*not exp.*	9	Great Western
77	Swindon................	both	1 27	53½	—	53½	—	„
220	Torquay	d.	5 12	42½	35	47¾	7	„
175	Wakefield	up	3 40	47¾	9	49¾	3	Great Northern
182¼	Warrington	„	4 25	41¼	22	45	5	Lon. and N.Western
202	„	„	4 42	43	23	46¼	6	Midland
219½	„	d.	5 28	40	31	44¾	9	G.N. and M.S. & L.
168	Weymouth	up	4 20	38¾	38	*not exp.*	7	Great Western
244¼	Whitby	d.	6 25	38	36	42	11	G.N. and N.E.
755¾	Wick	„	23 10	32½	180	*not exp.*	47	L.and N.W., Caln., and Highland
194	Wigan	„	4 34	42¼	18	45½	4	Lon. and N.Western
141	Wolverhampton..	„	3 4	46	7	48	2	Great Western
120	Worcester	„	2 58	40½	18	45	4	G.W. (*viâ* Oxford)
121½	Yarmouth	up	3 21	36¼	16	*not exp.*	4	G.E.(*viâ* Colchester)
124¼	Yeovil	d.	3 1	41	12	44	5	Lon. and S. Western
188	York	both	3 55	48	6	49¼	1	Great Northern

* Rhyd-ddu, 2¼ miles from summit.

† Snowdon, Strome Ferry, and Wick are given as out-of-the-way places.

These are the statistics of English expresses for the year 1883.
In this list there is no mention of the scores of rapid trains which
swarm between *Manchester* and the towns within 15 miles of it, of
those between *Glasgow* and *Paisley*, between *Derby* or *Nottingham*
and *Chesterfield*, between *Birmingham*, *Wolverhampton*, and *Stafford*,
between *Leeds* or *Skipton* and *Bradford*, between *London* and

Croydon, or in the neighbourhood of other busy centres. These distances are too small and the routes too crowded to give room for real express speed.

People sometimes complain of our present speeds that they are little if anything better than they were thirty years ago. What they mean is that the *very quickest* train to a given place may not be much quicker than it was. But whereas that quickest train used to stand apart in solitary distinction, the quickest now has dozens that almost touch its own high speed. And while the *number* of expresses has increased enormously, there has been a still greater increase in the crowds of goods or mineral trains through which they have to push their flight. Again, on our great lines the *average punctuality* has increased as well as (in some cases as much as) the average speed. The trains of which we hear such fond reminiscences, those myths of a railway Golden Age that never was, how did they behave *when the weather was against them?* Besides, how long had they to wait at stations (our own trains can rarely get away at their proper time, on account of that modern *bête noir,* luggage), when there was no straggling crowd of third-class clients to stop for? And then, the *weight* of these fast trains thirty years ago. Three or four, and scarcely ever more than six, little carriages, instead of the ten to fifteen half as big again which replace them to-day. Each mile of speed above 40 miles an hour represents now twice as much performance as then.* But, finally, it will be very hard to find even these cases (*Southampton* is the one) in which the one bit of high speed years ago is not yet topped. In Mr. Bellows's admirable French Dictionary there is a map of England, in which the time from London by quickest train is printed against the name of each chief town: nearly all these had to be altered on the issue of the 2nd edition in 1877, only two or three years after the first.

We have given no systematic list of "parade runs" on special occasions, for these are usually short trains, and have little effect on the every-day public services.

A few lines may be added to the above figures.

First, they represent the programme of the various Companies *on paper.* This programme is so good that it should be an object of each man's pride to carry it out every day in practice. But some lines do this better than others, generally those that set themselves the hardest task.

---

* For instance, in the year 1847, when Mr. Gooch's 8-foot engines were first placed on the G.W.R., *the* express was timed to *leave* Didcot (it stopped there) 57 minutes after departing from Paddington; and the distance—53 miles—was repeatedly run in from 47½ to 50 minutes. But how many carriages had this train? generally two.

Secondly, it is true that these figures would be more interesting if we had a history of them for several decades past, so that we might see the record of growth. In the meantime we may say roughly, that during the last 10 years the *mileage* of our express trains has increased about 30 per cent., and their average *speed* about 2½ miles an hour, while the *weight* of the trains has increased from 30 to 50 per cent. in many cases. (Third class passengers came into expresses generally about 1873.) This has taken place during a long-drawn depression of trade, and is perhaps one of the *sequelæ* of that depression (cheap materials.) It brings out however the pleasant fact that industrial dulness has not demoralized the excellence of workmanship in those industries essential to a railway.

Lastly, even apart from a retrospective comparison, the interest of these figures is obvious. The mileage and speed of express trains in England is so much greater than in the rest of the world, that any reflection on the fact must send a glow of satisfaction through every Englishman. For what is implied by this superior speed? We quote from the address by Mr. Percy Westmacott to the Institute of Mechanical Engineers at their meeting in Belgium last July, an address entitled "High Speed and High "Workmanship:"—

"Mechanical energy increases as the square of the speed; and "so it may be said that the mental energy and skill required to "carry on work increases also at something like the square of the "speed with which that work is performed. The materials used "must be far stronger and far finer; everything must be well "proportioned and balanced; there must be the most perfect "arrangement in each structure and in every part of a structure; ". . . . and thus we may say . . . . 'The higher the speed, the "'better the work,' for rapidity of working brings out and perfects "the highest qualities of the engineer."

And not only of the engineer, but equally of every man concerned in the working of the line, when railways are in question. There would be many fewer accidents on our lines altogether if the speed on *some* of them were higher, or if there were *more* of the highest speed. A low standard of requirement breeds a slack discipline, but when a company tries every day to run as well as it possibly can, there must be and is a devotion to detail all along the line.

As to the subtler, but not less valuable, social effects which result from quick transit, they are becoming too apparent to require pointing out. We may simply conclude with the answer of Mr. Frederick Barry before the Lords' Committee on the London and Birmingham Railway Bill (1832), that, as locomotion is a means to an end, "I take it as common sense that *the greater the* "*expedition, the more benefit will be derived by all parties,* where "certainty is to be had." For quick certainty of attainment, alike in the case of railways, justice, or anything else, is what makes the world throb with vigour.

APPENDIX.

———

(With regard to *William Hedley* a few extracts are here appended, taken from Mr. Archer's book).*

From HAYDN's *Dictionary of Dates.*

"WILLIAM HEDLEY, of Wylam Colliery, made the first travelling engine (locomotive), or substitute for animal power, 1813."

From WOOD, on *Railways, 1st edition,* 1825, p. 135.

"It was, however, a question of the utmost importance to ascertain if the adhesion of the wheels of the engine upon the rails was sufficient to produce a progressive motion in the engine when loaded with a train of carriages, without the aid of any other contrivance, and it was by the introduction and continued use of them upon the Wylam railroad that the question was decided."

From the *British Almanack for* 1837.

"It is a singular and instructive fact in the early history of locomotive carriages, that their projectors assumed the existence of a difficulty which is now known to be altogether imaginary; and that they set their ingenuity to work for the discovery of means for overcoming the presumed obstacle, without ever judging it necessary to ascertain, as they might have done, by very simple means, either the reality of the difficulty, or its degree, if it should be found to have existence. They assumed that the adhesion of the smooth wheels of the carriage, upon the equally smooth iron rails, must necessarily be so slight that if it should be attempted to drag any considerable weight the wheels might indeed be driven round, but the carriage would fail to advance, because of the continued slipping of the wheels, or, at best, that a considerable part of the impelling power would be lost through their partial slipping. As a remedy for this supposed evil, Trevithick provided, for the rims or tyres, projections similar to the heads of nails, or otherwise made their surfaces uneven by cutting in them transverse grooves. Following up this provision, he further proposed that wherever, as in ascending elevations, any greater

* *William Hedley the Inventor of Railway Locomotion on the Present Principle.*—(Newcastle-upon-Tyne, J. M. Carr, 1s.)

amount of the evil was to be apprehended, additional claws or nails should be projected from the rims of the wheels, in order more effectually to take hold of the road. A more elaborate invention was made the subject of a patent by Mr. Blenkinsop in 1811. This consisted of a rack placed on the outer side of the rail, into which a toothed wheel worked, and thus secured the progressive motion of the carriage. Another contrivance for this purpose was a chain placed along the road between the two rails, and passed over a wheel under the centre of the carriage, provided with upright forks to catch the links. The friction of the chain caused a great waste of power, and this contrivance was soon abandoned. The more ingenious idea of machinery which by its motions should imitate the action of the hind legs of a horse, and thus secure the progress caused by the engine, was taken up by several clever men, and for some years was the object of their inventive powers. One gentleman of considerable engineering talent who had succeeded, to his own satisfaction, in providing substitutes for the hind legs of a horse, carried his idea of imitating nature so far that he tasked himself to the production of a pair of front legs also; and he had already made great progress in the composition of his factitious horse, when the discovery was made that all these contrivances were needless, and that nature, in this case, required not any imitation, having herself provided, by an immutable law, that the adhesion of the wheels with the surface of the rails upon which they are moved is amply sufficient to secure the advance not only of a heavy engine, but an enormous load dragged after it."

From Locomotive Engineering, by ZERAH COLBURN, *London*, 1871,
p. 16.

"Hedley, acting for Mr. Blackett, was no doubt the first to work up the adhesion of the driving-wheels upon a commercial scale."

From the Steam Engine and its Inventors. ROBERT L. GALLOWAY,
1881, pp. 219 and 220.

"The many schemes which were on foot to effect locomotion by steam caused the year 1813 to be a memorable one in the history of the locomotive engine. Three locomotives, each acting on a different principle, were set to work on three different colliery railways on the north side of the River Tyne—Messrs. Chapman's chain-engine, on Heaton Colliery railway; Hedley's smooth-wheeled engine on Wylam Colliery railway; and one of Blenkinsop's engines, on the Kenton and Coxlodge railway.

" Regarding Messrs. Chapman's engine, it need only be remarked that the chain was found to give rise to great friction, and the engine to be very liable to get out of order, on which account it was soon abandoned."

Page 221.

" It was by the introduction and continued use of smooth-wheeled engines on the Wylam railway, that the absence of the necessity for any further aid than that supplied by the adhesion of the wheels to the rails was satisfactorily demonstrated."

From the History of the Growth of the Steam Engine, by Professor THURSTON, *1879, pp. 182 and 183.*

" This carriage was loaded with heavy masses of iron, and attached to trains of coal wagons on the railway. By repeated experiment, varying the weight of the traction carriage and the load hauled, Hedley ascertained the proportion of the weight required for adhesion to that of the loads drawn. It was thus conclusively proven that the weight of his proposed locomotive engine would be sufficient to give the pulling power necessary for the propulsion of the coal trains which it was to haul."

From a Letter signed " Justitia " in the Mining Journal, 6th October,
1860.

" In 1812, William Hedley, of the Wylam Colliery, demonstrated, upon a working scale, that the mere friction of the wheels of a heavy carriage upon the smooth rails of a tramway was sufficient to enable it to draw a train of loaded wagons, and by the early part of 1813 he had constructed a steam locomotive upon this principle, which was then and there put into working use for drawing the coal from the pit's mouth to the river.

" In 1814, George Stephenson, after repeatedly inspecting William Hedley's engine at Wylam, constructed an engine himself at Killingworth Colliery for Lord Ravensworth, which was employed in drawing coal wagons, as in the last named instance."

From the Illustrated London News, 15th October, 1864.

" On the south side of the Museum are a couple of locomotive engines—old, very old—worn, bent, bruised and rusty, but full of interest; for one is the oldest locomotive engine in existence, the parent of all that have since been produced, the original old ' Puffing Billy,' of the Wylam Colliery, constructed there in 1813 by William Hedley."

From the National Encyclopædia. MACKENZIE, *London,* 1864.
Article : "*Locomotive.*"

"After various inventors had long exerted their ingenuity in vain to give the locomotive a firm hold of the track by means of roughened wheel tires, rackwork rails, and toothed driving wheels, legs and feet, and other contrivances, William Hedley, in 1813, made the important discovery that no such aids are required, the adhesion between smooth wheels and smooth rails being sufficient."

From the Times, 21st *January,* 1865.

"In this engine, the two great features which made the locomotive a success were first applied—the sufficiency, for traction, of the smooth rail and wheel, and the steam blast up the chimney. The sufficiency of the smooth rail and wheel for traction was, indeed, the great principle, the establishment of which rescued the locomotive from oblivion. The only means by which heavy loads could be drawn by locomotive power before Hedley's time was by the employment of the toothed wheel and the racked rail, as introduced by Blenkinsop and Trevithick, but 'the pull' tore up the racked rail, and consequently this system had to be abandoned for horses."

From Mr. ISAAC LOWTHIAN BELL'S *Paper on The Tyne as connected*
with the History of Engineering, read before the Members of the
Institution of Mechanical Engineers, at their Annual Meeting,
held at Newcastle-upon-Tyne, 2nd *August,* 1881.

"For forty or fifty years the horse on the level, and the steam engine, by means of ropes, on uneven ground, continued to labour on our iron roads in the conveyance of coal to its point of destination ; when a crude idea of Trevithick's was taken hold of by Mr. Blackett, of Wylam, near this town, who, with the aid of his engineer, William Hedley, constructed the first locomotive which ever did any work worthy of the name."

From MICHAEL REYNOLDS'S *Model Locomotive Engineer,* 1879.
P. 106.

"The locomotive, at this very period, was generally in great disrepute. In many ways it had improved, but, after all, it was a costly article. A good deal of this was caused by Stephenson himself not availing himself of the best boiler at first. In 1828, he employed a return-flue boiler, as Hedley had done in 1815. Here we have twelve years in which the best boiler was disregarded. The complaint was always that there was a want of steam. It was an enormous sacrifice on the part of Stephenson to ignore Hedley's boiler for so extended a period."

From the Life of GEORGE STEPHENSON. WARD, LOCK, & CO., *London,* 1881.

"Mr. Hedley made the important discovery, by experiment, that a smooth rail would offer sufficient friction to enable the wheels of an engine to advance upon it, if the weight of the engine was made proportionate to the load it had to drag; and that the rack rail and toothed wheels were therefore unnecessary. It had always been thought that engine wheels on a smooth surface would 'surge' or slip round without advancing."

From the Liverpool Mercury, 12th July, 1882.

"The fact has been as clearly established as the tradition is inveterate, that it is to William Hedley, of the Wylam Colliery, near Newcastle-upon-Tyne, and not to George Stephenson, that we are indebted for the modern locomotive. Stephenson was the man who took the invention in hand, and who, with such prestige as it gave him, combined with the added force of his own great genius, pioneered and developed the railway system. But Hedley was the man who made Stephenson's work possible; for it was he who discovered that a locomotive with smooth wheels, running upon smooth rails, would draw weights far heavier than itself, who invented the return-tube boiler, and who carried the exhaust pipe into the chimney and upturned it therein . . . . . These were subsequently adopted by Stephenson—the smooth wheels in 1814, the carrying of the exhaust pipe into the chimney in 1815, and the return-tube boiler in 1828. During all this intervening period— from 1813 to 1828—Hedley's engines were working economically and well. These facts have been stated over and over again on isolated platforms, and in the by-corners of books and magazines but we have never seen them brought out so clearly as they are in a small volume by Mr. M. Archer, recently published by Mr. J. M. Carr, at Newcastle-upon-Tyne. The book contains diagrams which will materially assist the letterpress in showing clearly what was the precise nature of Hedley's contributions to an invention which has revolutionised transit throughout the civilised world. It also gathers up and groups together the scattered testimony in support of Hedley's claim. The volume therefore is a very interesting one, and will be highly valued by all who desire to be accurately informed with regard to the railway locomotive."

From the Bristol Mercury and Daily Post, 12th June, 1882.

"Once upon a time, whilst on an angling excursion on the picturesque banks of the Tyne, a few miles above Newcastle, our ruminations on the vexatious coyness of the finny tribe were disturbed by a sound of a subdued roaring, apparently at no great distance. . . . . . It turned out that we were confronting 'Puffing Billy,' the first locomotive engine that had ever been successfully worked, and which was then, at an age of more than forty years, as perfectly fulfilling its purpose as when it was placed on the rails. Dr. Smiles's memoir of George Stephenson being at that time in the full bloom of its popularity, the story of the engineman seemed incredible: but curiosity led to further inquiries, and the result brought us to conclusions substantially identical with those embodied in this book. . . . . . That all this should be little known except in the immediate locality is due to the fact that Mr. Hedley regarded his engine as an incidental matter of his business, and, in becoming a large colliery proprietor and shipowner, had his attention turned to other matters; whereas Stephenson, assisted by the Peases, became the head of a locomotive manufactory, gradually introduced various improvements, and was identified with most of the early passenger railways. None the less just, however, is Hedley's claim to be the father of the locomotive."

Industry, 16th June, 1882.

"The father of the modern locomotive." In an ably compiled *brochure* recently published, Mr. M. Archer, of Newcastle-upon-Tyne, vindicates the title of the late Mr. William Hedley, of Wylam, to this honourable distinction.

"[The reviewer here sketches the history of Trevithick's unsuccessful attempts to make a workable locomotive, also of the arrangements tried by Blenkinsop, by Chapman, and by Brunton, then describes Hedley's experiments to test if smooth-wheel traction would answer all purposes, and remarks as follows:—]

"From that hour the railway locomotive was ushered into the domain of practical mechanics. To Hedley undoubtedly belongs the honour of originating the idea, and of testing its soundness by effective experiments. He also built the first really good engine on this principle, and although it proved weak for lack of faculty of generating steam, yet a few months after, in May, 1813, a second engine was built by him, and this proved eminently successful. This is the celebrated 'Wylam Dilly,' which, well battered in hard service, may be seen at the South Kensington Museum. It is important to note that this engine was provided with a return-tube boiler, and had the exhaust pipe carried into the chimney and up-turned therein. Many modifications and improvements in minor points have doubtless since been introduced, but, in all its first principles, the locomotive remains the same as Hedley made it."

.   .   .   .

" Stephenson's successful construction of locomotives for the Killingworth Colliery was, in order of time [1814 and 1818] sub-sequent to Hedley's success, and in point of merit Stephenson's early specimens were decidedly inferior ; his success, in fact, was only partial and relative. The smooth wheels were there, for no man in his senses would have wished or have dared to return to the abandoned cog wheels and supplementary and similar devices.

" But Stephenson's boiler was on Blenkinsop's principle ; there was no blast in the chimney, and the chimney was three times the area of that of Hedley's engine. It is a notorious fact, that during the building of Hedley's engine, Stephenson frequently walked across the country in the evenings, from Killingworth to Wylam, and studied the construction of the new machine, and there can be no doubt he so far followed that construction in building his own engine as to disentitle him to the claim of absolute originality.

" Stephenson was, in point of fact, the disciple and pupil ; Hedley was the master, and Stephenson's first engines were equal to Hedley's only so far as the pupil followed the master. When he diverged into originality he travelled into error, and came back to right principles of construction only as he returned loyally to the teaching he had received. Moreover, it is decidedly true that by his temporary defection from Hedley's plans of construction, Stephenson delayed the early development of railways and retarded his own success. *It is a fact not generally known, that at one time, owing to many partial failures, the locomotive was in great disfavour, and, except in Hedley's experiments, was regarded as a failure down to* 1828, *or thereabouts.* There were, indeed, serious thoughts of abandon-ing all hopes of making it complete, and of returning to the use of horses. It was Timothy Hackworth, of Shildon, who, at the solicitation of the shareholders of the Stockton and Darlington Railway, set about constructing the ' Royal George,' which began to work in 1827. He adopted the general features of Hedley's locomotive   .   .   .   .

By his successful labours he rescued the locomotive from the neglect and disrepute to which it had been consigned. He was an able man, and has left the impress of his genius on the Stockton and Darlington Railway, but he has never received his due share of honour. But whatever credit belongs to Timothy Hackworth, it is a reflection from William Hedley, for Hackworth served under Hedley, at Wylam, and a loyal and enthusiastic pupil he was, and though less famous he was more original, at least in his construction of the locomotive, than was Hedley's other pupil, Stephenson. Those who have seen the early locomotives in actual work will remember the clumsy head gear by which they were disfigured, but which at the time were considered essential to their working. To Hackworth we are indebted for disburdening them of these grotesque and unnecessary superincumbrances. His 'Royal George' appeared without them in 1827, as did also all the new constructions after that date, and thenceforth the power was transmitted more directly and more efficiently to the driving wheels. It is remarkable that the proper meed of praise and the proper share of emolument have not been awarded to the several pioneers and inventors connected with the noble enterprise, the development of the locomotive. Stephenson has had all the honours without having contributed by any means all the originality and merit. Cugnot became miserably poor, Trevithick was left forsaken, a poverty-stricken wanderer, Hackworth was overlooked and neglected when the rewards of success went round; and Hedley, the real father of the modern locomotive, was eclipsed by the brighter glare of his pupil's fame. Posterity will do its best to rectify those wrongs of contemporaries; but the reputation of Stephenson as a man of genius and of high personal character will be none the less extremely brilliant when others receive their due. The Quakers of Darlington, and the establishment of Stephenson's locomotive manufactory at Newcastle under the Quakers' auspices, and with their capital, first opened out the career of Stephenson; the extraordinary development of the railway system throughout the civilised world completed that career. That career was too grand to require meretricious brilliancy by filching the fame that belongs to others. It has been said that, but for Stephenson and his locomotive, Sir Rowland Hill would not have been possible. With greater propriety and truthfulness it may be said that, but for Hedley, Stephenson himself would not have been possible. It was a great thing for Stephenson that he should have been indispensable to railways, penny postage, and the widespread success of the locomotive in every land; it was a greater thing for Hedley that he should have been indispensable to Stephenson, and all that was involved in his wonderful labours and career."

HARRISON AND SONS, PRINTERS IN ORDINARY TO HER MAJESTY, ST. MARTIN'S LANE.